AMERICAN PATCHWORK DESIGNS IN NEEDLEPOINT

AMERICAN PATCHWORK DESIGNS IN NEEDLEPOINT

Melanie Tacon

Guild of Master Craftsman Publications Ltd

First published 1998 by
Guild of Master Craftsman Publications Ltd,
166 High Street, Lewes, East Sussex, BN7 1XU

Photographs by Zul Mukhida
Line drawings by Simon Rodway

ISBN 1 86108 088 3

Designed by Teresa Dearlove

Set in Times Roman and Gill Sans

Colour origination by Viscan Graphics (Singapore)
Printed in Hong Kong by H & Y Printing Ltd

Dedication

This book is dedicated with love to my nephew and niece Josh and Beth Tacon.

Acknowledgements

My thanks go to the following people: first and foremost to my mum Mary McCallum, who has been through the whole experience with me; to Liz Inman and her team at GMC Publications, particularly Stephen Haynes for his patience, and seamless editing; to Zul Mukhida for the photography; to my family and friends for their unfailing support, interest, and encouragement; and finally to Gill Thompson and Pat Manchee who between them opened my eyes to the beauty of patchwork.

Measurements

Although care has been taken to ensure that metric measurements are true and accurate, they are only conversions from imperial. Except for very small dimensions, they have been rounded up or down to the nearest 5mm (0.5cm), or to the nearest convenient equivalent in cases where the imperial measurements themselves are only approximate.

Contents

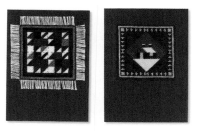

Part Two: How to Do It

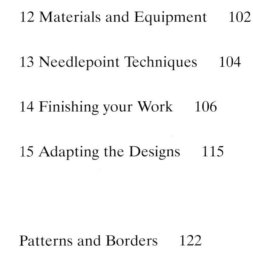

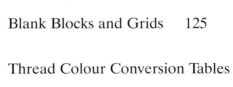

1 Introduction

Textiles and their endless combinations of colours, patterns, and textures have fascinated me from a very early age. As a toddler in Manchester, I was surrounded by beautiful fabrics. The family business was a small factory manufacturing quilts, which in those pre-central heating days were deep, fluffy, feather-filled eiderdowns, topped with jewel-coloured, machine-embroidered satin or with paisley prints, and backed with cotton. Unlike today's duvets, they fitted the dimensions of the top of the bed, and were used in conjunction with matching bedspreads, on top of sheets and blankets. The contours of those quilts became the mountains and valleys of imaginary lands, which – with stories and plays on the radio – sparked more adventures than a lifetime of videos ever could.

My parents gave me my first sewing machine – a much loved hand-cranked Singer – for my tenth birthday, and from the age of about twelve, dressmaking was second nature.

Growing up in the sixties and seventies when hippies and flower power brought about revivals in dressmaking and crafts like macramé, crochet, tie-dyeing, patchwork, spinning, and weaving, gave me the opportunity to try out many different techniques.

Between 1975 and 1978 I was nanny to a little girl in south-west France. The couple I worked for – a doctor and his wife – were (and still are) wonderful people, always treating me more like a younger sister than an employee. Apart from one brief period, I didn't live in the house, but in a series of three different apartments in the village, which sits on top of a hill in the department of Aveyron, on the south-west corner of the Massif Central. The views from my apartments were stunning: it was like living on the roof of the world. It was during that time that I taught myself tapestry weaving – mostly landscapes – and then went back to rediscover and explore canvas embroidery, which is far less time-consuming, but has similar textural qualities. I have never looked back.

I am a passionate stitcher. My idea of true bliss is a six-hour train journey through France, travelling in first class, and conveniently next to the buffet car. I am probably the only person working in London who considers herself fortunate to have a daily two-hour commute in each direction. I stitch anywhere and everywhere – buses, waiting rooms, parks, planes, and trains.

The room I use as my studio at home is light and full of colour, with large baskets brimming with wool, a pine chest which holds rolls of canvas and fabric, a pinboard covered in postcards, bits of wrapping paper, half-stitched sample pieces, bits of woven landscape, a pair of bookshelves stuffed with scrap albums, magazines, books, and boxes of all those things that 'normal' people throw away.

Generally, I design by stitching directly onto the canvas. By the time I start to stitch, I have a pretty good idea in my head of what I'm trying to achieve, but it's only by stitching a sample piece that I can tell whether the colours and shapes work together. For fiddly bits, such as corners, I use graph paper and coloured pencils, and although I do have a computer, it is really only used to chart a design after stitching.

Patchwork is a craft I have always admired but until fairly recently had avoided, for two reasons: ignorance, and fear. My experience of patchwork, from the seventies, was of paper templates and endless hexagons, or of Suffolk Puffs and Cathedral Windows, which are great fun to do, but have very little practical application. Later, when I discovered how little I actually knew, I hesitated to let it get hold of me, because I didn't think we had the storage space to cope with the then inevitable collection of fabrics.

It was in Brittany on a textiles course, one Easter about four years ago, that my eyes were finally opened. The students on the course were able to choose from a number of different disciplines, one of which was patchwork, and as the week progressed I was astonished by the diversity of things I saw growing before me. When I got home again I determined to do some research and read about patchwork, its history and development – particularly in America.

2 History

The origins of patchwork are often disputed. Every continent of the world can show ancient artefacts which are held up to be early examples of the craft. Realistically, however, going back to the basic meaning of the word, patchwork has existed from the first moment that man learned to join the skin of one animal to that of another.

In Europe, until the foundation of the East India Company in 1600 and the advent of relatively cheap imported calico and chintz from India, cloth was either home-made and extremely labour-intensive, or purchased at great expense. Even in wealthy households, fabric was prized, and patchwork was developed as a frugal, yet decorative way of using or recycling every small scrap.

By the time the first European colonists arrived in America, the patchwork quilt was already a well-established article of their household bedding. It was a combination of circumstances and skill which changed the European-style quilts into the designs we now recognize as American patchwork.

Most people have only the vaguest idea of how hard life really was for the first settlers, and many are unaware that the first English colony was not founded by the 'Pilgrim Fathers' in Massachusetts, but 13 years earlier in what became Virginia.

In the spring of 1607, in the reign of King James I of England (VI of Scotland), three English ships sailed into Chesapeake Bay, and landed at the mouth of the James River (loyally named for the king). Lured by explorers' tales of a Utopian paradise, a place of milk and honey, where crops grew and harvested themselves, and rich lands that were there for the taking, this small bunch of slum-dwellers, sailors, convicts, and young men in search of fortune and adventure were totally unprepared for what awaited them. Of the original group of 105 who had survived the voyage, more than half died of pneumonia or starvation during the first winter. Bad weather prevented further supply ships from reaching them, and they had neither the skills, nor – it seems – the inclination to repair or replace the things they had brought with them. The supplies

were gone within seven months. The local Indians – at first friendly and curious – understandably became hostile and resentful when the colonists started to steal their crops. When it became too dangerous to forage in the surrounding forest, the Englishmen were driven to chop up their own cabins for firewood.

After two years, only 38 people remained alive. Admitting defeat, they packed up what was left into one of the ships, and were preparing to set sail for home when they met an incoming ship loaded with more supplies and colonists. The settlement was saved.

Self-sufficiency became the name of the game, and shirkers were no longer tolerated. John Smith – one of the original group – became their self-appointed leader, and ruled the colony with the simple biblical rule 'He that will not work, neither shall he eat.'

After years of privation and hardship, the salvation and future of the Virginian colonies was found in the form of an Indian crop which grew like a weed. This was tobacco, and later – with the cultivation of sugar cane, cotton, and indigo – it formed the economic basis of the huge plantations and estates of the Southern States.

By 1733, thirteen English colonies had been established along most of the length of the Atlantic coast. In European terms, this is roughly the same distance as from Aberdeen in Scotland to Rome in Italy, and has as many variations in terrain, but with more pronounced extremes in climate.

The speed at which the settlements grew and spread inland contributed in no small way to demand for household goods outstripping supply. In 1760, Vermont's estimated population was 300. A mere 31 years later, it was more than 85,000.

Each colony had its own government, currency, and unique mix of population, but all were faced with the same domestic problems.

Right from the earliest days of colonization, the English government imposed protectionist trade and tax laws such as the Navigation Act, which not only banned trade, except with England, but also tried to prevent the colonies from becoming self-sufficient.

Production of textiles was strictly forbidden. It was illegal for anyone trained in the textile industry to emigrate, and the mere possession of a spinning wheel carried the drastic penalty of having one's right hand cut off.

Of course, in practical terms, these laws were unenforceable. In 1640, in direct and open defiance, Massachusetts and Connecticut decreed that every house must grow a certain amount of flax, and that each household must spin three pounds of wool, flax, or cotton per week, with a fine of one shilling levied for every pound-weight shortfall.

Sheep became highly prized, and new settlers were encouraged to bring more with them from Europe. It was made illegal to export ewes, and at one point, the inhabitants of Philadelphia swore not to eat lamb.

After the War of Independence, supplies from Europe more or less dried up for a while, and until the new American textile industry was established – the first cotton-spinning mill did not open in America until 1793, in Rhode Island – precious cloth became even more valuable.

Against the background of all these hardships – poverty, climate, illness, taxation, and war – the pioneering women raised families, tended crops and animals, spun and wove cloth from which was made the family's clothes, linen, blankets, and quilts.

The most important innovation of this period was the idea of making the quilt from manageable lap-sized pieces, rather than as a huge sheet. These pieces became the block designs we recognize today as American patchwork.

American patchwork designs translate wonderfully well into needlepoint. Both techniques are endlessly flexible in terms of scale and colour combination. In this book, I have collected just a few traditional designs, and hope to show readers how these can be used and adapted to create a range of items which will be both beautiful and practical. Projects range in size from 1½in (4cm) to 18in (46cm) square, and are suitable for stitchers of all levels of skill from complete beginner to very experienced.

Part One
The Projects

Before you start

If you are new to needlepoint, you should read the general instructions in Chapters 12 and 13 before attempting any of the projects. Instructions for finishing your work and making it up into cushions and other articles are given in Chapter 14.

The instructions in this book are intended to be as flexible as possible, so that you can adapt each project according to your own taste. This is why the project instructions for cushions, for example, do not specify cushion pad sizes or border widths: you should simply make up the cushion to the size you prefer, using any of the methods described in Chapter 14.

You can also scale the designs up or down as required, and even customize the designs themselves, by changing a plain patchwork to a patterned one, adding plain or patterned borders, or devising your own colour scheme. Advice on this is given in Chapter 15, and on pages 122–46 you will find a selection of fabric and border patterns which you can use, and black-and-white grids of the patchwork patterns to assist in planning colour schemes.

Using the charts

The charts in this book are in colour and, wherever possible, the printed colours are representative of the actual threads used. Occasionally, however, where two neighbouring colours are similar, it has been necessary to exaggerate the colour contrast on the chart.

The projects in the photographs have been stitched with DMC threads. Tables showing the nearest equivalent shades in Anchor threads are given on page 147, but please note that it is not always possible to give exact equivalents.

Each square on the chart represents one stitch, except where otherwise stated. Where a stitch other than the ordinary tapestry stitch has been used, this is explained in the project instructions.

Thread quantities

The amounts of thread given in each project key are approximately what you will need to finish the item using the basketweave version of the needlepoint stitch (see page 105). If you choose to use one of the other methods of stitching described on page 104, you will need roughly half as much. Every stitcher has a different tension but, as a rough guide (which is also useful when designing your own projects), an 8-metre skein of wool will cover 10 square inches (65cm^2) using tent stitch, or 5 square inches (32cm^2) using basketweave, on 12-gauge canvas.

3 Squares

The early settlers had arrived with no idea of how harsh the American winters would be. Underprepared and undersupplied, the only way they had of replacing and adding to their household linen was by improvisation. Feed sacks were roughly pieced together with any available scraps of cloth to form quilts which were stuffed with leaves, grass, raw wool and cotton, or shredded paper. When these wore out, they were used in turn as filling for newer quilts.

Rectangles and squares were randomly pieced at first, to form a crude sort of 'crazy patchwork', and then patterns such as bricks and chequerboards began to emerge.

The two projects in this section are both simple designs made from squares.

Happy Scraps
Chequerboard pincushion

This design can be made to cover any area, and is really useful for using up little scraps and leftovers of thread.

Method

Stitch the navy chequerboard pattern first, then fill in with the other squares, either following the chart or using your own choice of colours. If you choose to adapt the pattern to your own needs, all you need to do is expand it. The non-navy squares are randomly placed; the chart and the photograph show only two of the infinite possibilities.

Refer to pages 111–12 for advice on adapting needlepoint to a circular shape.

Variations

Choose your own alternative colour scheme with (say) dark green instead of navy, with pinks, reds, and oranges used to fill in the randomly coloured squares.

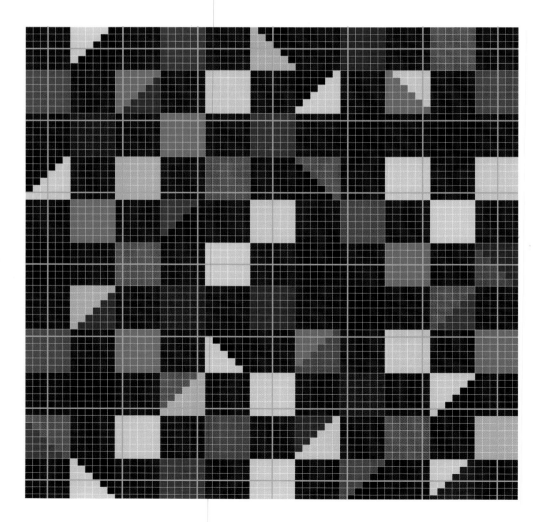

Materials

9½ x 9½in (24 x 24cm) 12-gauge canvas

DMC tapestry wool in the following quantities:		
Colour	**No**	**Skeins**
Very dark navy blue	7308	3
Emerald green	7943	1
Light emerald green	7909	1
Pale green	7954	1
Very pale green	7604	1
Dark blue-green	7860	1
Turquoise	7650	1
Bright turquoise	7995	1
Deep violet	7247	1
Purple	7245	1
Lilac	7708	1
Lavender blue	7791	1
Pale blue	7313	1

Apart from the dark navy, the longest length required of any of the above colours is about 27in (about 70cm).

Sunshine and Shadow
Scissors keeper

The Amish and Mennonite communities have had a tremendous influence on American patchwork. They have made quilts (always by machine) since about 1860. Their own traditional designs are bold geometrics characterized by large areas of dark, sombre shades enlivened with surprisingly quirky accents of brilliant colour, and they bring the same originality to their interpretation of other, more widespread designs.

This pattern is also known as Trip Around the World, or Granny's Dream.

Method

Begin stitching in the centre of the design as usual, making sure that the ends of the wool are well secured.

To make up the scissors keeper, follow the instructions for a plain cushion on page 109.

Variations

As the scissors keeper is so tiny, you could enlarge the size of the squares to 3 x 3 or 4 x 4 stitches and make a matching pincushion or needlecase without having to purchase extra thread.

Alternatively, you could attach it to a key-ring.

Materials

5 x 5in (12.5 x 12.5cm) 12-gauge canvas

DMC tapestry wool in very small amounts of the following colours :

Colour	No
Royal blue	7319
Very pale blue	7800
Pale blue	7798
Lavender blue	7245
Pale mauve	7709
Deep pink	7208
Pink	7759
White	Blanc
Medium sea green	7596
Dark green	7329
Muddy green	7417

4Stripes

Each square patch was not necessarily cut from a single piece of cloth, but could be made up of several separate fragments to achieve the required size and pattern. Simple striped blocks were the next logical step, and two of the designs featured in this chapter, Cats and Mice and Fence Rail, are good examples of these.

Quilts made by piecing broader strips of cloth, such as the Amish Bars pattern, or the 'strippy quilts' so characteristic of the north of England, became popular after the advent of the sewing machine. Deceptively simple in design, these quilts were mostly made by women who liked to show off their quilting skills. Each strip would be quilted with plaits, feathers, chevrons, or more naturalistic designs like vines, leaves, or flowers.

Amish Bars
Herb sachet

This is a classic Amish design, with its use of black and dull green, with small highlights of brighter orange and sharp citrus yellow.

The proportions of this design are important. The central bars are always half the width of the outside border, and twice the width of the inner border.

I have used black coton perlé to add a slight lustre and textural contrast, but you could use tapestry wool if preferred.

Method

Stitch the central bars first, beginning with the middle rust-coloured stripe. The rest of the design should then fall easily into place.

Make up the sachet following the instructions for a plain cushion on page 109. Fill with your own choice of herbal mix or potpourri, in a separate gauze bag if appropriate.

10 x 10in (25.5 x 25.5cm) 12-gauge canvas

DMC threads in the following colours and quantities:		
Colour	**No**	**Skeins**
Black coton perlé no. 3	Noir	6
(or black tapestry wool	Noir	5)
Rust	7169	2
Green	7364	1
Lemon yellow	7785	1
Orange	7439	very small amount

Variations

Although the balance of the design should not change, and the traditional colour to use for the dark areas is black, you can create some stunning combinations with dark brown, navy, charcoal grey, maroon, or bottle green, combined with contrasting, electrically bright colours.

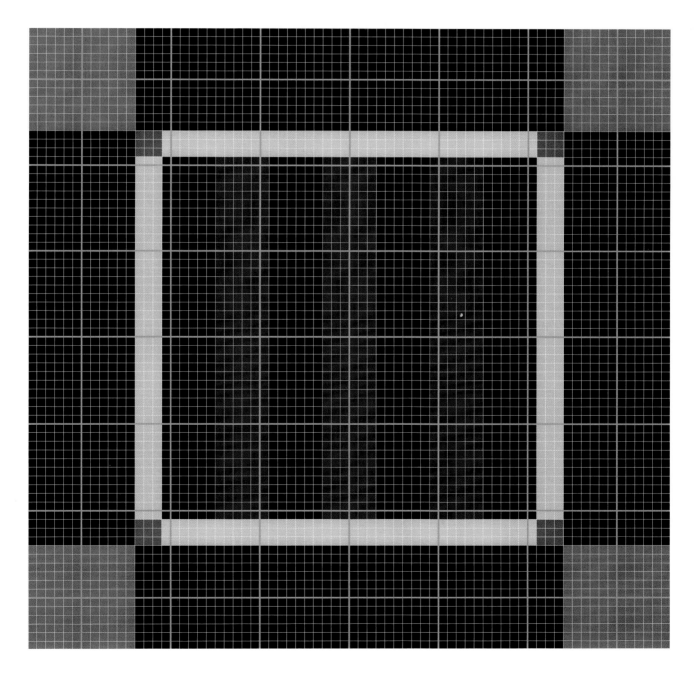

Fence Rail
Curtain tieback

This design is said to represent the shadows made by the sun falling on a picket fence.

Method

Rather than starting in the middle, you can work this project left to right, rolling up the finished piece as you go. A cardboard tube, such as the inside of a roll of kitchen paper, slit down its length and slipped over the work, will help to keep it clean.

Variations

This pattern is most commonly found using three shades of the same colour, but you could just as easily use three contrasting colours, or even introduce several more into the pattern.

Materials

7 x 26in (18 x 66cm) 12-gauge canvas

DMC tapestry wool in the following colours, 1 hank of each:

	Colour	No
	Dark green	7428
	Mid-green	7385
	Pale green	7402

NB: If your stockist does not have hanks of wool, they will be able to advise you on the number of skeins you need to complete the project.

The required length of your curtain tieback will depend on the size of your curtains. The quantities above are sufficient to make one 22in (56cm) long and approximately 3½in (9cm) wide.

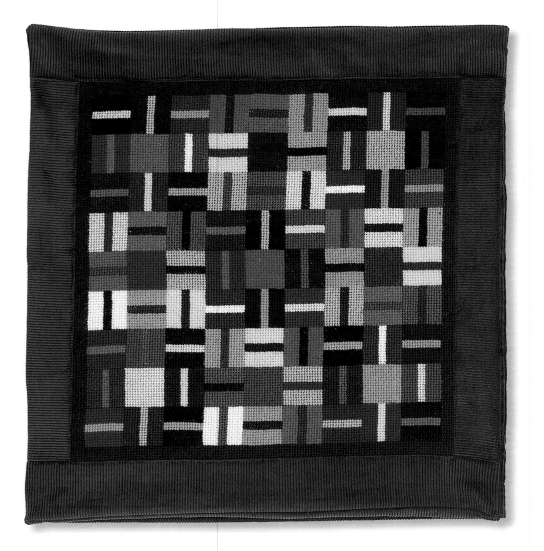

Cats and Mice
Cushion

The 'Liquorice Allsorts' cushion, as my mother christened this design, is made from a very simple nine-patch block. Again, the proportions are important: the middle stripe of the outside blocks is always half the width of its neighbours.

Before you start

If your sewing tension is a little tight, you may find that the darker colours do not cover the 10-gauge canvas as well as you would like. If you think there is any danger of this, you would be well advised to substitute 12-gauge canvas, and either add a couple of plain coloured borders to make up the required size, or set the work into a fabric border. Alternatively, some suggestions for patterned border designs can be found on page 122.

Method

Begin stitching with the hot pink square at the centre of the design.

Single block

Finished size: approx. 4½ x 4½in (11.5 x 11.5cm)
Key square (see page 115) = 15 x 15
Central square   approx. 3yd (3m)
Outside patch, main colour   approx. 2yd (2m)
Outside patch, stripe   approx. ½yd (0.5m)

Whole cushion panel

19 x 19in (48.5 x 48.5cm) 10-gauge canvas

DMC tapestry wool in the following colours and quantities:		
Colour	No	Skeins
Dark brown	7469	5 (=1 hank)
Shocking pink	7602	1
Claret	7212	2
Navy blue	7307	2
Custard yellow	7055	2
Bright gold	7436	2
Dark sea green	7860	2
Medium sea green	7596	2
Dark rust	7184	2
Black	Noir	2
Hot pink	7106	1
Burnt orange	7360	2
Teal blue	7306	2
Dull gold	7474	1
Very dark brown	7535	2
Cream	Ecru	1
Dark grey-green	7999	2
Ice blue	7298	2
Apple green	7547	2

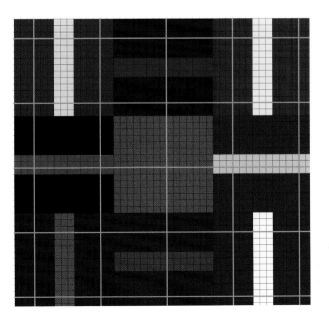

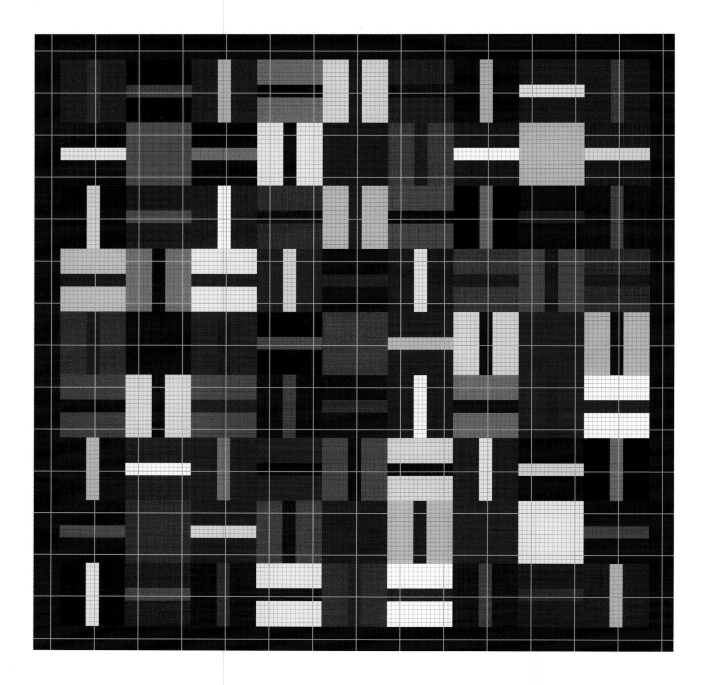

Cats and
Mice
Pincushion

The blue and yellow pincushion shown here is exactly the same pattern as the full-sized project, but with the patch size reduced to its minimum for this design, 5 x 5 stitches. With a reduced colour palette, it almost gives the appearance of woven ribbon.

Method
As for Cats and Mice cushion (see page 14).

Materials

7 x 7in (18 x 18cm)10-gauge canvas

	DMC tapestry wool in the following colours, I skein of each:	
	Colour	**No**
	Medium sea green	7596
	Teal blue	7306
	Cream	Ecru
	Custard yellow	7055
	Bright gold	7436
	Dull gold	7474

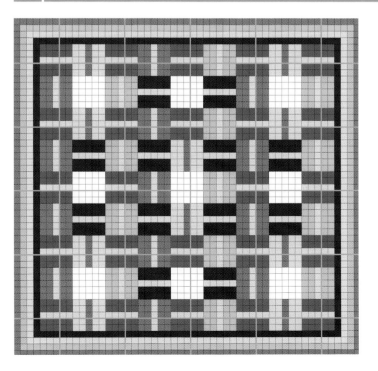

5 Log Cabin

The group of designs known as 'Log Cabin' are amongst the oldest and best-known of all patchwork patterns. Although the exact origin is unclear, examples are known to have existed for at least 200 years in America, Canada, Scandinavia, and northern Europe.

Stitched directly onto a piece of backing fabric, the basic block is formed by surrounding a central square with concentric strips, arranged in different patterns of dark and light according to the chosen variation. The foundation square is usually made of calico or wool, depending on the required weight of the finished article, but as this method of construction means that log cabin designs are 'self-quilting', wadding is seldom added. The stabilizing effect of the backing fabric also allows different weights of cloth to be used in the same piece, which in pioneering days was both practical and thrifty, and today enables modern quilters to experiment with textures such as velvet, silk, and brocade.

Traditionally, the central square of each block is red, representing the hearth and heart of the cabin, with the 'logs' in patterned or plain shades of brown, russet, green, gold, and cream. Amish Log Cabin designs – particularly the Pineapple variation – are often quite mind-blowing in their use of dark and bright primary colours, giving the whole pattern a three-dimensional, psychedelic, whirling effect.

Random Log Cabin
Box top

Although I have provided a chart for this project, the idea of Random Log Cabin is that you can use up scraps of thread to fill any size. For my box top, I drew a line around the area to be filled, then stitched a small red square in the centre, and other red oblongs scattered across the canvas with no particular pattern. These formed the foundation squares for the Log Cabin blocks, and I stitched strips of varying widths around them, alternating warm and cool colours. The narrowest strip is only one row of stitches, the widest is six stitches deep.

Method

Begin stitching with the red square in the centre of the design, and sew each block separately.

Materials

8½ x 10⅓in (21.5 x 26.5cm) 18-gauge canvas

	Colour	No
	DMC coton perlé no. 5 in the following colours (1 skein of each):	
	Red for centres	666
	Claret	814
	Strawberry red	347
	Raspberry pink	309
	Lemon	307
	Gold	783
	Warm brown	355
	Bronze	920
	Apricot	922
	Pale mushroom	738
	Navy blue	336
	Bottle green	890
	Deep aqua	924
	Pale aqua	926
	Mid grey-blue	931
	Very pale blue	809
	Dark mustard	781

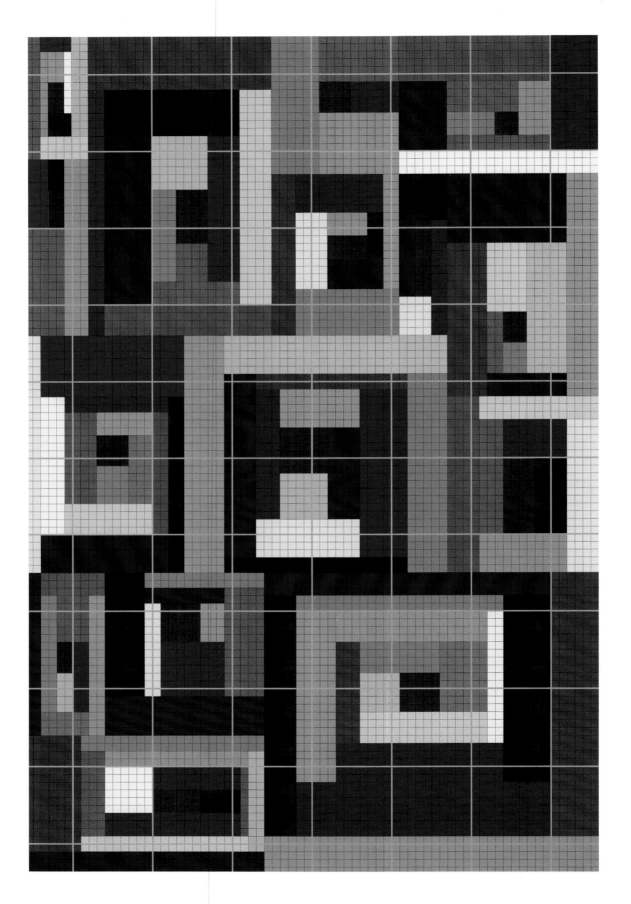

Pineapple Log Cabin
Wall hanging

The pineapple is a symbol of hospitality, and quite a few old quilts worked in this variation have survived, because they were saved for use by visitors, and not used on a day-to-day basis.

I am fortunate enough to work in a building that has views across the Thames to St Paul's Cathedral in one direction, and Westminster in the other. At lunch time there are several quiet places in the South Bank arts complex where I go to sit, stitch, and watch the world go by.

As that area attracts a great many tourists, I occasionally get to meet visitors to London, who, having spotted me in my corner, wander over to find out what I am doing. A group of Americans stopped to talk to me when I was stitching this wall hanging, and I was delighted when at least two of them turned out to be quilters and recognized the design. So, for the ladies from Wisconsin, this is the finished article – I hope you still like it!

Method

The first chart shows a quarter of the whole design; the second chart shows the placement of all nine blocks. Begin stitching with the red diamond in the middle of the centre block, and stitch each block separately.

Variations

I chose to make this into a wall hanging, and hang it diagonally, rather than square, because I feel this enhances the stained-glass effect of the colours I have used, but you could just as easily make it up into a cushion or a bag. Pineapple Log Cabin is not a quiet, gentle pattern. It lends itself to really wild colour combinations, and you can achieve all sorts of effects, full of whirling movement and vitality.

19 x 19in (48.5 x 48.5cm) 12-gauge canvas

DMC tapestry wool in the following colours and amounts:

	Colour	No	Skeins
	Dark blue	7297	15 (= 3 hanks)
	Royal blue	7319	3
	Hyacinth blue	7030	3
	Turquoise	7595	3
	Mustard yellow	7782	2
	Lemon	7679	2
	Bright yellow	7785	5
	Red for centres	7108	6
	Claret	7110	5
	Shocking pink	7600	5
	Orange	7947	3

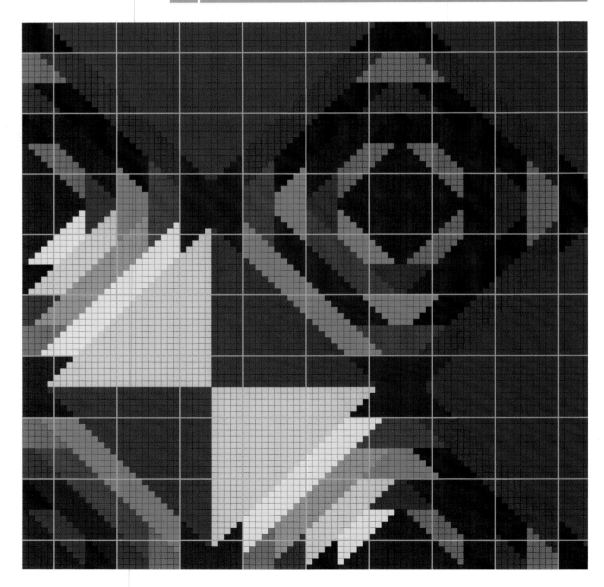

6 Irish Chain

The patterns which fall into this group are very simple, but extremely effective. Their origins seem to be debatable – in Ireland they are sometimes known as American Chain – but they are widespread and very popular.

The traditional colours – at least in Europe – are white with turkey red and/or green, but the Amish and Mennonite communities in adopting these designs inject their own bold colour schemes.

Often, as in all their work, these devout people will include a deliberate mistake in their patchwork – a wrongly coloured square, or a gap in a border – as their acknowledgement that only God is capable of creating perfection. This belief carries through to all levels of their lives. They shun the use of modern things, preferring to live in an uncomplicated, unadorned manner: using horse-drawn buggies rather than motorized transport, candles and lamps instead of electricity. Even the dolls that the Amish children play with, although clothed in a traditional manner, have no faces.

Double Irish Chain
Cushion

I have used the basic Double Chain pattern for this cushion, but with the option of using a textured stitch to add tactile interest. Double Irish Chain looks quite complicated, but in patchwork terms, it only uses two blocks.

Method

Start with the rust square in the centre of the lattice, and work outwards to each corner to form a large X. I have used triple rice stitch (see Fig 13.5 on page 105) for all the brown and terracotta squares (each block of 4 x 4

stitches on the chart represents one triple rice); but you could always replace this with tent stitch if you prefer. After that, the rest of the design should fall into place fairly easily. All the cream sections should be stitched in your chosen method of tent stitch, and it is best to leave them to the end so that they stay clean, but as I've said before, the object of the exercise is enjoyment, so if you feel a little daunted by stitching so much of one colour, you can fill in the cream as you go.

Needlepoint has suffered in the past from

the reputation of having vast amounts of background to fill in – what some call the 'All that beige!' syndrome. This design and the Star of Bethlehem project are the only two in this collection which have large areas of a single colour, and in stitching them you may find it less tedious to assemble as many needles of the right size as possible, thread them all up, and leave them in a pincushion ready for use, so that you can have a good long session without having to break your rhythm to reload the needle. It also helps to have a good movie on television or a play on the radio.

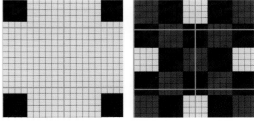

Materials

18 x 18in (45.5 x 45.5cm) 10-gauge canvas
Key square (see page 115) = 4 x 4

	DMC tapestry wool in the following colours and quantities:		
Colour		**No**	**Hanks**
Terracotta		7920	2
Dark brown		7533	3
Cream		7579	3

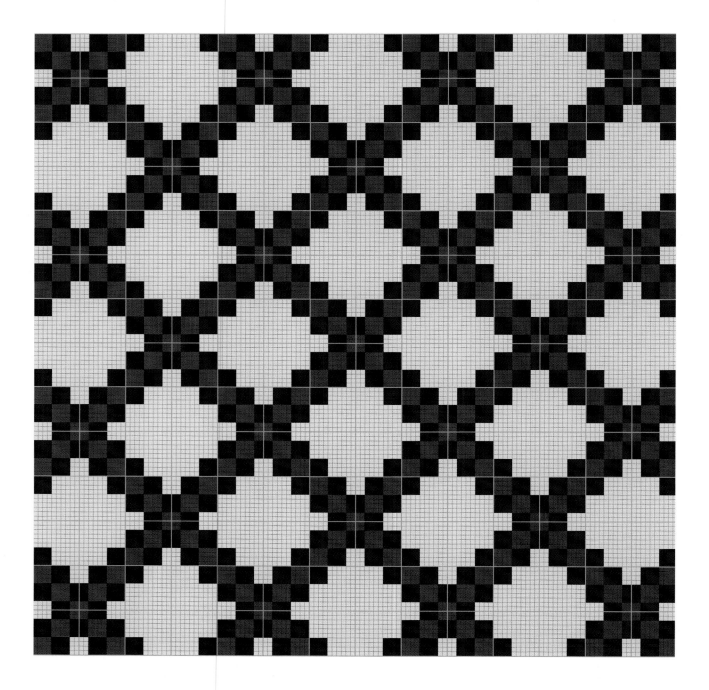

Irish Chain, Snowball Variation
Needlecase

This is very similar to the Double Chain design, and can be used in many different ways. To illustrate this, here is a needlecase which shows the pattern in two different sizes. One version reduces the pattern to its smallest possible extent, with each patch of the nine-patch block measuring only two stitches square, whilst the other is scaled up to three times that size. The larger version of the design reminds me of a medieval heraldic banner, hung from the walls of a great hall, which is why I have used these deep, rich colours. The long-legged cross stitch used around the edge is ideal for this sort of project, as it forms a natural edging when the canvas is turned under. Instructions for this are on page 105.

Method

Begin stitching in the centre of the larger version of the pattern, and complete that side of the case before stitching the small-scale lattice.

Variations

As well as the two-stitch and six-stitch versions of this pattern, you could use blocks of three, four, or five stitches to adapt the pattern to the size you require, and use it for any project of your choice.

Materials	8½ x 13in (21.5 x 33cm) 12-gauge canvas		
	DMC tapestry wool in the following colours and amounts:		
	Colour	No	Skeins
	Claret	7110	3
	Bright gold	7056	3
	Bronze	7780	4

Irish Chain with Flowers
Scented sachet

Many old quilts are appliquéd with a red or pink flower known as the Rose of Sharon. This project is not a true patchwork pattern, but a very stylized adaptation of that sort of quilt, and uses an Irish Chain-type lattice in rice stitch to add textural interest. The cream background and the dark centres of the flowers are stitched in wool, the flower petals, leaves, and lattice in coton perlé. The lattice and flower centres are stitched in rice stitch, which is explained in Fig 13.4 on page 105, but you could replace this with tent stitch if you wish.

Method

Start by stitching the lattice, beginning at the centre and radiating out until the rest of the design falls into place. For the lattice and the flower centres, each block of 2 x 2 squares on the chart represents one rice stitch.

Make up the sachet as for a plain cushion (see page 109), and finish with purchased lace or trimming if desired.

Variations

This pattern would make a lovely ring pillow, or a cover for a photograph album to commemorate the wedding of friends. You could replace the flower in two of the central diamonds with the initials of the bride and groom, put the date in the other two, and then expand the trellis and rose pattern to the required size, perhaps altering the colours to match the bride's bouquet.

Materials

9½ x 9½in (24 x 24cm) 12-gauge canvas

DMC threads in the following colours and quantities:			
	Colour	No	Skeins
Tapestry wool:			
	Cream	7746	7
	Dark red	7198	1
Coton perlé no. 3:			
	Blue-green	991	1
	Bottle green	890	2
	Pale green	987	1
	Deep pink	326	1
	Bright pink	601	1

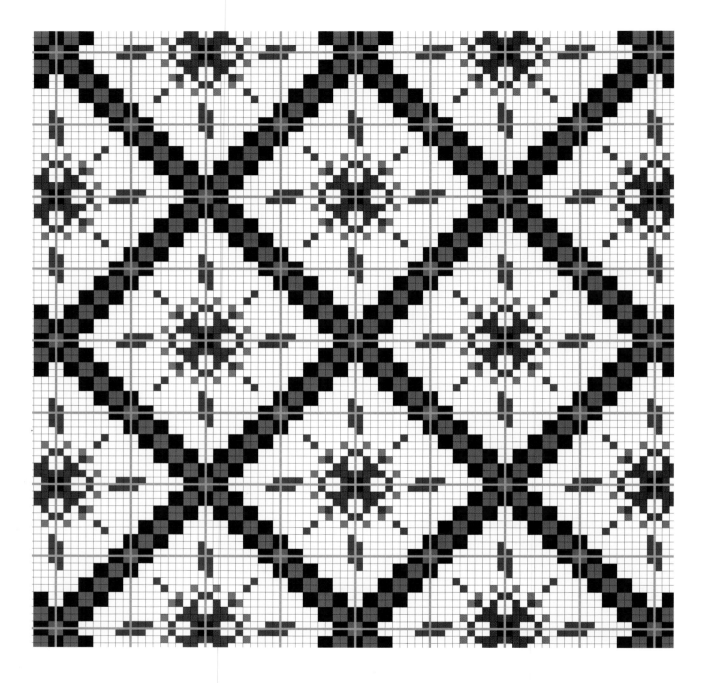

7 Flora and Fauna

As Philadelphia, Baltimore, Boston, New York, and the other cities down the eastern seaboard became larger, more sophisticated, and prosperous, the frontiers were pushed west. After about 1750, settlers started to move inland in great numbers to claim more land.

Their possessions had to be easily transportable, and even if she spent all day in a wagon, a woman still had to make clothes and quilts for her family. It was at this time that the American block method of patchwork really came into its own. Once all the pieces had been cut out, a large quilt could be made in lap-sized units which could be stitched on a wagon, round a camp fire, or – once built – in a tiny cabin.

Early log cabins would initially have consisted of just one room with a beaten earth floor, and windows which were either open, or covered with oiled paper or pared-down animal skin, and protected from the elements at night with wooden shutters. In this room the whole family lived, ate, and slept. Small children would share a large bed with their parents, while the older ones slept on pallets which would be stored under the big bed during the day. Quilts for the main bed were large enough to fall to the floor on all sides, so that the pallets could be hidden from view.

All the projects in this chapter have names relating to plants and animals. Block names derive from all sorts of things: the name of the maker, their location, some aspect of agricultural or religious life, or sometimes an event or person of historical importance. Many blocks have more than one name, having been handed down through family and friends in communal quilting bees, and then taken by travelling salesmen or wagon train to more remote locations.

A good example of this is a block called Jacob's Ladder by the Puritan communities in New England, which became the Road to Oklahoma and then the Road to California as settlers moved further west. As a general rule, the longer a block has been around, the more names it has.

Maple Leaf Rug
Card

Although needlepoint is usually
stitched on canvas, it works very
well on other even-weave fabrics,
such as linen. This design has
areas of the linen left uncovered,
and illustrates a different
approach from the other projects
in the book. The linen is softer
than canvas, with a slightly
nubbly weave, and uniquely (in
this collection) I used a round
embroidery frame to stabilize the
fabric before stitching.

Method

Stitch the design using two
strands of thread throughout,
and use one strand for the
'quilting' stitches (marked with a
heavy black line on the chart)
which separate the four blocks.
Next, remove the linen from the
frame, and, placing it right-side
down on a towel, cover with a
clean, damp cloth and press out
the creases caused by the frame.
Measure the stitched area and
cut a piece of very lightweight
iron-on interfacing to fit. Iron
this onto the back of the stitched
area to stabilize it. Cut the linen
to within ½in (1.25cm) of the
stitching, and carefully pull away
the individual threads to form a
fringe. Leaving the fringed area
free, glue the stitching carefully
to the front of your card. Place a
piece of clean paper on top, and
weigh down with a heavy book
until completely dry.

Variation

For a more textured effect,
substitute coton perlé no. 5 in
the same colours, using sewing
cotton for the 'quilting' stitches.

Materials

6 x 6in (15 x 15cm) square of 18-count rough-weave linen
Very lightweight iron-on interfacing to fit
Key square (see page 115) = 7 x 7

DMC stranded cotton in the following colours (1 skein of each):

	Colour	No
	Claret	814
	Brown	975
	Bronze	356
	Orange	922
	Raspberry	3350
	Purple	327
	Red	347
	Bright red	349

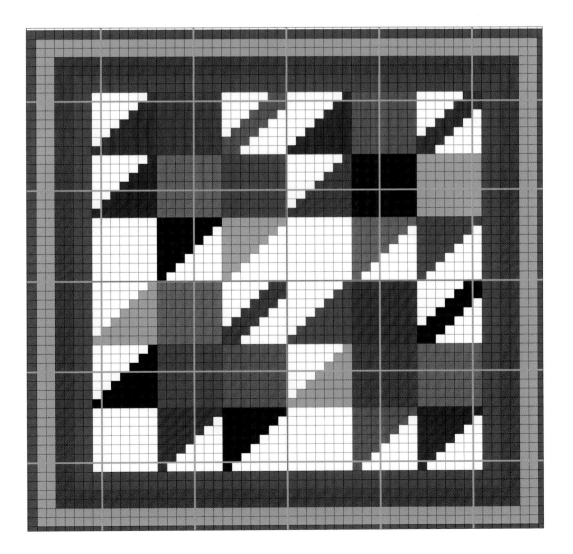

Tessellated Maple Leaf
Cushion

When I was a child, we had a puzzle called a 'Magic Square' which came in the form of small triangles and rectangles of thick, unglazed terracotta pottery. It had an instruction sheet which contained silhouettes of various things – animals, birds, and geometric shapes – and the challenge was to duplicate these shapes by placing all the pieces together in a sort of mosaic, without any being left over. This patchwork pattern reminds me of that puzzle, in the way each leaf shape slots precisely into its neighbours, like a piece in a jigsaw puzzle. Although it is composed of simple nine-patch blocks, each leaf shape is incomplete on its own.

Method

Begin stitching in the centre of the design, where the two green leaves meet the red and lemon.

Variations

If you omit the black border, this design is exactly the right size for a glasses case when folded in half sideways. You will need to replace each of the black triangles with the appropriate colour to make the pattern continuous when you stitch the side and bottom seams.

Materials

14 x 14in (35.5 x 35.5cm) 12-gauge canvas
Key square (see page 115) = 5 x 5

DMC tapestry wool in the following colours and quantities:			
	Colour	No	Skeins
	Red	7544	2
	Burnt orange	7360	2
	Apricot	7918	2
	Gold	7505	2
	Lemon	7973	2
	Green	7364	2
	Dark grey-green	7398	2
	Dark blue-green	7329	2
	Brown	7499	2
	Black	Noir	9

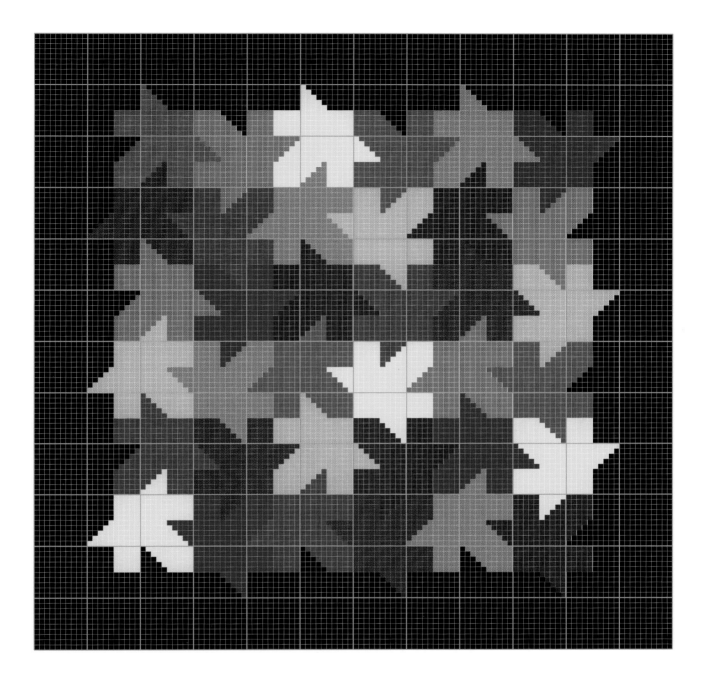

Shady Pines

The two projects in this section are based on medallion-style quilts, where a single central block is surrounded by a series of complementary borders.

Medallion quilts are often made as a group project, where one person will piece the central block, and the other stitchers will each add a border until the required size is achieved.

The two versions of this design differ only in the size of the key square – in this instance, the dark blue squares – and certain adaptations to the blue and gold striped border which forms the trunks of the pine trees.

Shady Pines
Coaster

Method

Begin stitching with the gold diamond in the middle of the design, then work the apricot star, and the blue and cream squares that radiate out to each corner. The rest of the design should then fall into place quite easily.

Materials

6 x 6in (15 x 15cm) 18-gauge canvas
Key square (see page 115) = 4 x 4

DMC coton perlé no. 5 in the following colours (1 skein of each):

	Colour	No
	Red	817
	Gold	783
	Apricot	922
	Dark green	986
	Navy blue	823
	Cream	746

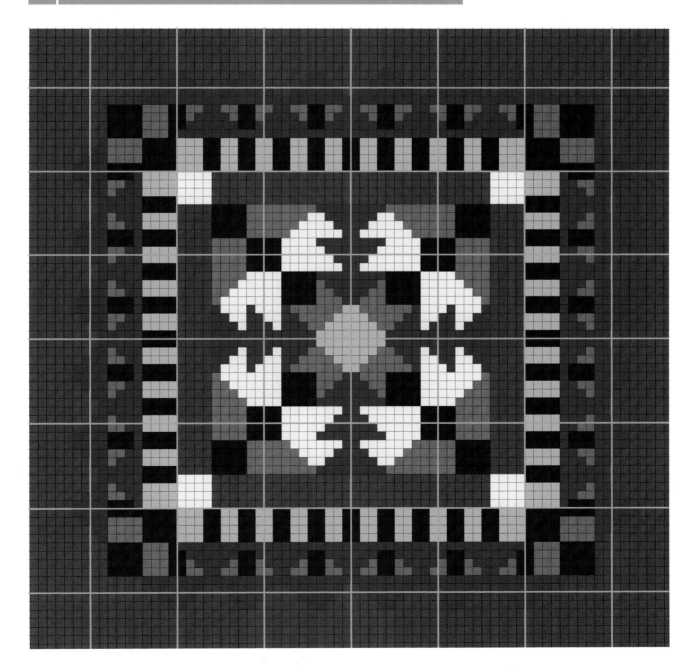

Shady Pines
Cushion

Method

Following the chart opposite, which shows a quarter of the design, begin with the gold diamond in the centre. For the whole design, refer to the chart on page 44.

Materials

21 x 21in (53.5 x 53.5cm) 12-gauge canvas
Key square (see page 115) = 12 x 12

DMC tapestry wool in the following colours and quantities:		
Colour	**No**	**Skeins**
Red	7108	20
Gold	7505	7
Terracotta	7920	8
Dark green	7389	12
Dark blue	7297	8
Cream	7503	5

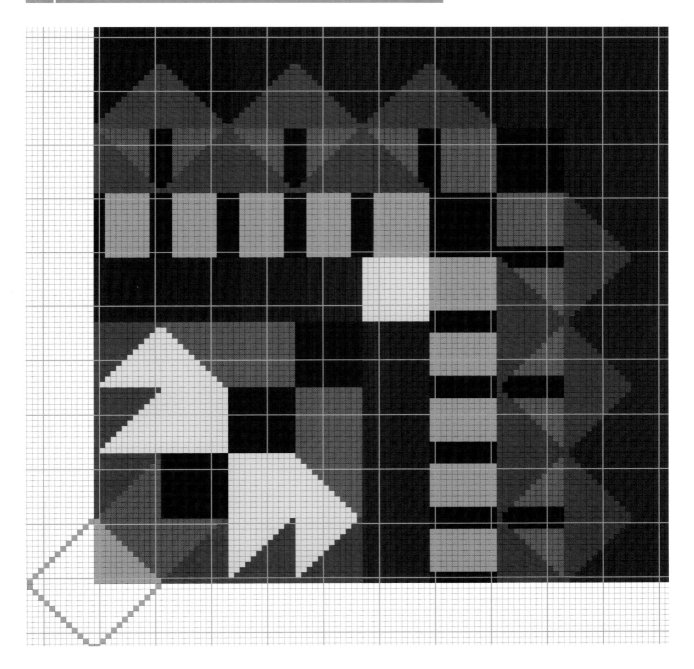

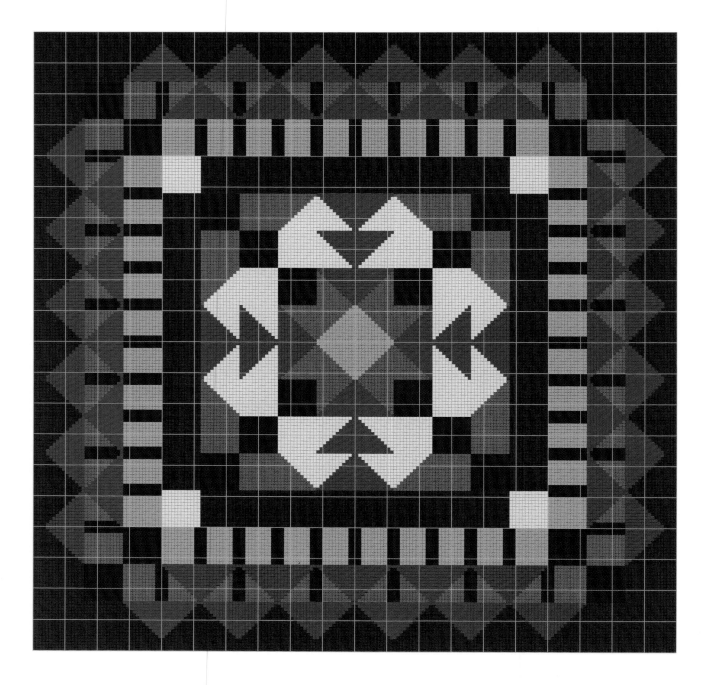

Bear's Paw
Card

This is another good example of a block with several names. Known as Bear's Paw on the wilder western frontiers, it was known at the same time as Duck's Foot in the Mud in more populated areas, and as Hands of Friendship by the Quakers in Philadelphia. The striped border is known as Chinese Coins.

Method

Begin by stitching the claret diamond in the centre of the design.

Variations

The reds I have used for the bear's paws are quite close in colour. Using a more contrasting colour for the 'claws' would make the design much spikier and more dramatic.

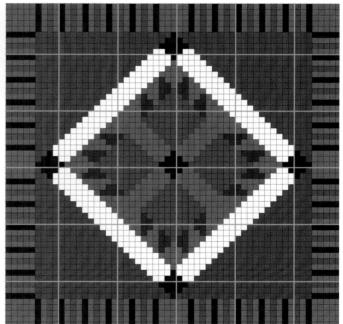

Materials	6 x 6in (15 x 15cm) 18-gauge canvas		
	DMC coton perlé no. 5 in the following colours (1 skein of each):		
	Colour	No	
	Bronze	920	
	Turquoise	806	
	Claret	814	
	Strawberry red	347	
	Bright red	349	
	White	Blanc	

Duck Paddle
Coasters

Making a gift for someone in needlepoint need not be vastly expensive or take a long time. With four skeins each of four colours, you will have enough thread to make a set of six coasters. These can be mounted in plastic coasters, which are widely available, or given a border of long-legged cross stitch and backed with felt.

I have used the colours I associate with the plumage of a mallard duck for this set, but you could use any combination of your choice.

Method

Depending on your working environment, you can stitch the set on the same piece of canvas, or split your canvas into six equal pieces.

Stitch each coaster separately, beginning with the centre.

Variations

Instead of stitching these blocks as separate coasters, you could join them up to make a larger project.

Materials

15 x 10in (38 x 25.5cm) 12-gauge canvas. If you choose to stitch all six coasters on one piece of canvas, you **MUST** allow a gap of at least 1in (2.5cm) between them.

A single coaster will need about 5 x 5in (12.5 x 12.5cm), and 1 skein of each colour. The quantities given below are for the set of six.
Key square (see page 115) = 7 x 7

	DMC tapestry wool in the following colours (4 skeins of each):	
	Colour	**No**
	Brown	7459
	Burnt orange	7360
	Dark green	7327
	Cream	7579

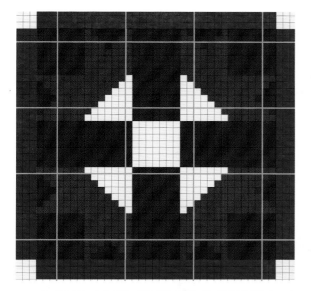

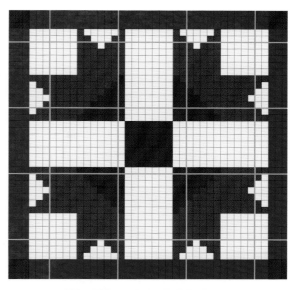

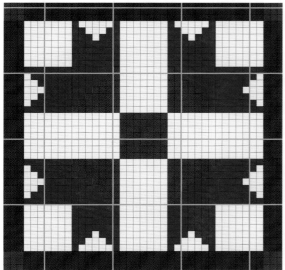

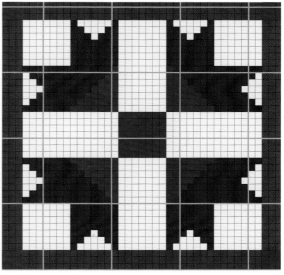

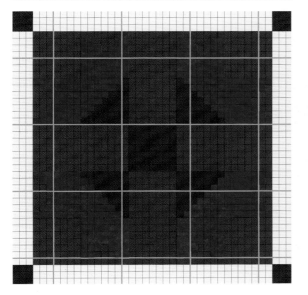

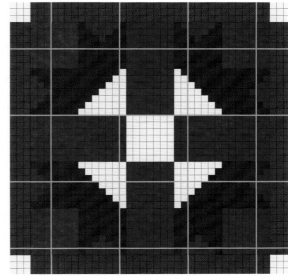

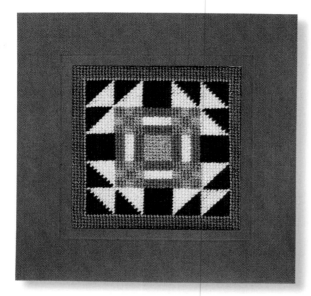

Goose in the Pond
Card

As with many of the blocks in this collection, Goose in the Pond lends itself beautifully to being mounted in a card. I wanted to use this as a Christmas card, so my goose is a Snow Goose, with sparkling metallic gold thread and brilliant white starkly contrasted with deep navy blue.

Method

Begin stitching in the centre. For areas stitched in metallic gold, use two strands of thread.

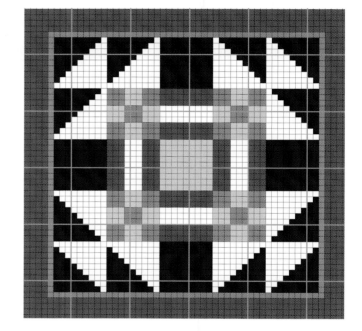

<table>
<tr><td rowspan="10">Materials</td></tr>
</table>

5 x 5in (12.5 x 12.5cm) 18-gauge canvas
Key square (see page 115) = 9 x 9

	DMC coton perlé no. 5 in the following colours (1 skein of each):	
	Colour	**No**
	Navy blue	823
	White	Blanc
	Bronze	780
	Gold	782
Metallic Stranded Cotton (1 skein)		
	Gold	

Goose in the Pond
Patterned cushion centre

I have used the patterned version
of Goose in the Pond as a
cushion centre, by using it as the
base square for a Log Cabin
block constructed in strips of two
shades of denim.

Method

Start in the centre of the design
with the yellow and white
patterned square.

Materials

12½ x12½in (32 x32cm) 10-gauge canvas

DMC tapestry wool in the following colours and quantities:		
Colour	**No**	**Skeins**
Royal blue	7318	4
Powder blue	7314	3
Bronze	7780	1
Yellow	7785	2
White	Blanc	2

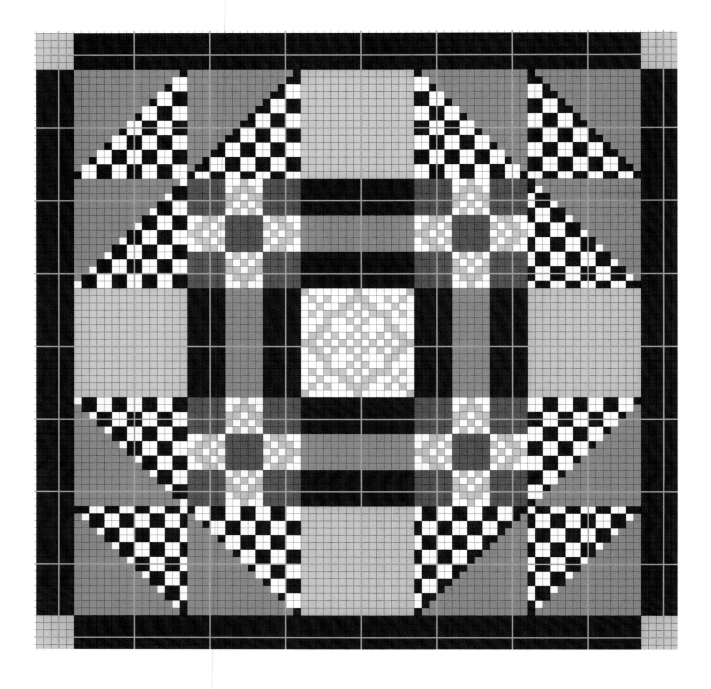

8 Stars

Paper became readily available from the mid-1880s, when it began to be produced from wood pulp rather than cotton or linen. Before this, patchwork block patterns were not passed from maker to maker as diagrams, but as actual fabric blocks – hastily cobbled together using scraps, sometimes from memory – and usually covered with handwritten notations. These were then stored, pretty much as we would keep photographs in a shoe box, or sketches in a scrapbook, until the right moment came to use them.

At the end of the nineteenth century, shortly after the improvements in paper production, came the first linotype machines, which immediately revolutionized the printing and publishing industries. Magazines and journals were mass-produced for the first time, and these soon became a popular source of block patterns, as quilt-makers swapped them through reader-to-reader advice columns.

In 1886 Sears, Roebuck and Co. launched their first mail-order catalogue, and the convenience of home shopping quickly caught on, particularly in rural areas, where expanding transport systems meant improvements in mail delivery times.

In 1889 the Ladies' Art Company was founded, and by 1928 their catalogue offered not only art needlework and sewing gadgets, but a library of some 530 patchwork block designs. These were available either as paper patterns or as actual sample blocks.

Stars are by far the most popular motif in American patchwork. As a symbol of human hope, expectation, and harmony, a stylized flower, and – of course – the motif chosen to represent each state on the national flag, the star can be found in dozens of variations, from the simplest six- or eight-pointed shape to the most spectacular starburst.

This chapter presents a total of 10 different star blocks, in 13 variations.

Ohio Star
Picture

This is one of the most basic star blocks, and is also known as Shoo Fly.

I wanted to find a decorative way of keeping a record of block patterns which included the name, and the 'Home Sweet Home' sampler-style frame works rather well.

Method

Begin by stitching the gold square in the centre of the block, the bottom of which should sit on the horizontal centre fold of the canvas. The actual centre of the design is in fact about 3 stitches lower, but with 2in (5cm) spare canvas all round, you do not need to be exact.

Variations

Almost any of the blocks in this collection can be displayed in this way. A set of three or four such pictures would look most effective hung as a group. Colour schemes can be adjusted to fit any decor, and the alphabet used here is given on page 136 for your use.

Materials

10 x 12in (25.5 x 30.5cm) 12-gauge canvas
Key square (see page 115) = 16 x 16

	DMC tapestry wool in the following colours and quantities:		
	Colour	**No**	**Skeins**
	Dark rust	7184	5
	Green	7379	1
	Brown	7449	1
	Orange	7946	1
	Gold	7783	1
	Pale yellow	7472	1
	Cream	7579	1

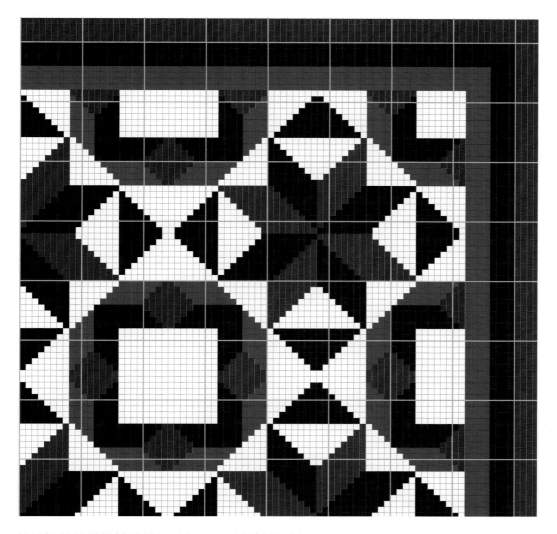

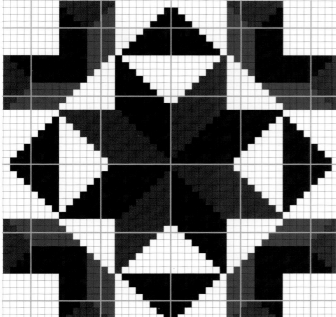

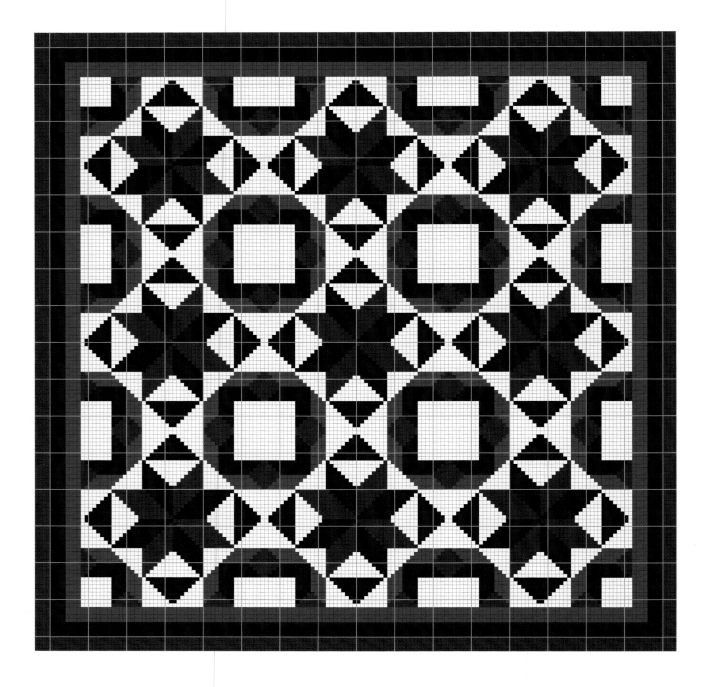

Martha Washington's Star

Two cushions

This, like the Ohio Star block, is one of the simplest star patterns, and it is the only full-sized design that I have stitched twice for this book, to illustrate how designs can be converted from plain to patterned, or vice versa.

Plain cushion

This cushion, with its gentle pinks and greens, is stitched for my French friend Paulette Santucci Bonnin, who sometimes finds my choice of colours a little 'shocking'.

Method

Begin stitching with the burgundy and cream pinwheel in the middle, and work each block separately.

Materials

Single block

5¼ x 5¼in (13.5 x 13.5cm) 12-gauge canvas
Key block = 15 x 15 stitches

	DMC tapestry wool in the following colours and quantities:		
	Colour	**No**	**Skeins**
	Cream	7492	4
	Pale green	7424	1
	Burgundy	7139	1
	Cerise	7137	2

Whole cushion front

20 x 20in (51 x 51cm) 12-gauge canvas

	DMC tapestry wool in the following colours and quantities:		
	Colour	**No**	**Skeins**
	Cream	7492	13
	Dark pine green	7408	12
	Pale green	7424	11
	Burgundy	7139	7
	Cerise	7137	10

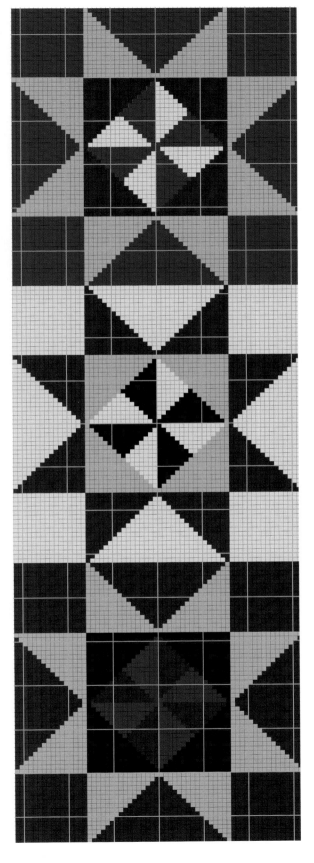

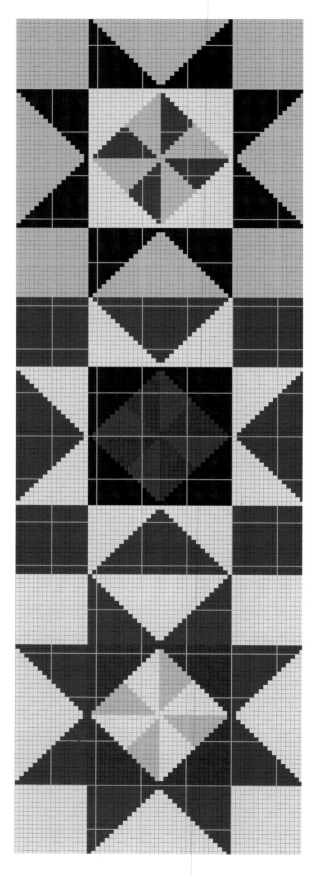

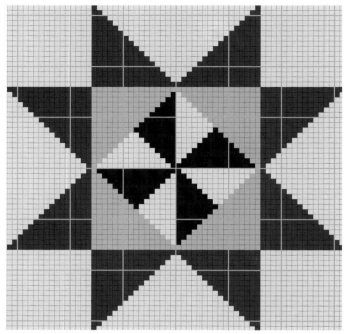

Martha Washington's Star
Patterned cushion

This cushion was great fun to design and stitch. If you are a new stitcher, you may find that using several colours in one area will make your work very thick and unwieldy. This is perfectly normal – do not let it discourage you. It may be preferable to use 10-count canvas rather than 12-count. This will make a big cushion even larger, but it will be much more pleasurable to stitch, and easier on the fingers.

I feel that the gingham fabric used for the borders and back of the cushion sets the design off very well, but you could replace it with another pattern or a plain colour, or make up the design as a borderless cushion; the choice is yours.

Method

When stitching a highly patterned area, it is easier to use half-cross stitch rather than the diagonal basketweave stitch (see page 104), as this makes the work less bulky on the back. Be careful not to pull your wool too tight when moving from one area to another, as this can cause your work to pucker.

Materials	20 x 20in (51 x 51cm) 12-gauge canvas		
	DMC tapestry wool in the following colours and quantities:		
	Colour	**No**	**Skeins**
	Burgundy	7147	6
	Cerise	7137	8
	Pink	7760	8
	Dark green	7389	7
	Mid-green	7320	8
	Pale green	7369	8
	Cream	Ecru	7
	Very pale apricot	7171	4

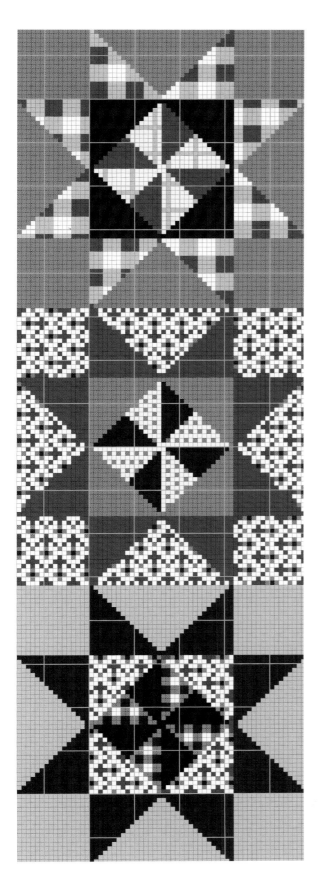

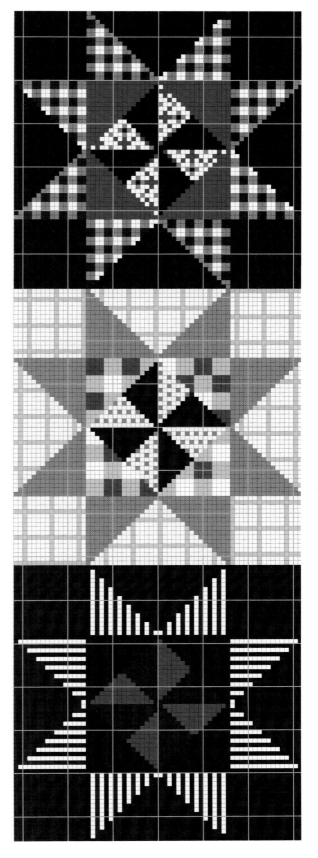

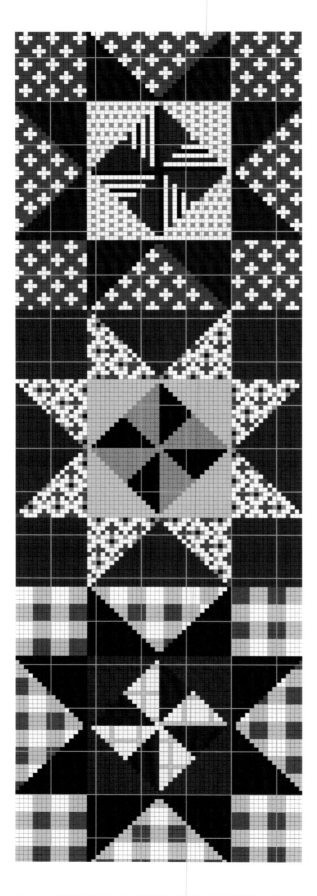

Dutch Rose
Footstool

Here is a design which can be adapted to fit various sizes of footstool, or which could be used for a church hassock.

This design is a real mixture of influences. The large, three-dimensional star is a classic patchwork pattern, which fitted my stool beautifully, and the border and background can easily be altered to fit your needs. The chequerboard background, with its tiny sparks of pink and white, is influenced by French medieval tapestries. The ribbon border is a recognized patchwork border, but also appears in the marble floor of St Mark's Basilica in Venice.

The stool frame I used has an aperture which measures 8¼ x 10¾in (21 x 27.5cm), but the stitched area is much larger to accommodate the padded top. You will almost certainly need to alter the pattern slightly to fit the frame you have; advice on this can be found on pages 115–17.

Method

Begin by stitching the central motif, leaving the cream sections until the end to prevent them from becoming dirty. Then, depending on the size of your footstool, you may need to alter the background and border to fit. If you need to change the corners of the border design, it is best to work it out on graph paper before you begin stitching, as you will have to think about what needs to happen to the design in the centre of each side, so that all the corners match.

Materials

14 x 16in (35.5 x 40.5cm) 12-gauge canvas
Key square (see page 115) = 10 x 10

DMC tapestry wool in the following colours and quantities:		
Colour	**No**	**Skeins**
Dark green	7329	11
Mid-green	7320	4
Dark pink	7961	4
Pale pink	7354	4
Cream	Ecru	2

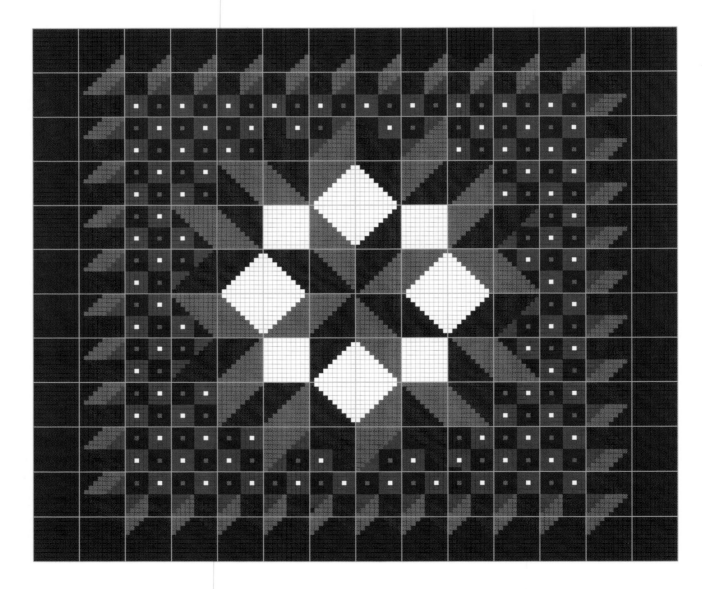

21 x 21in (53.5 x 53.5cm) 12-gauge canvas

DMC tapestry wool in the following colours and quantities:

Colour	No	Skeins
Black	Noir	30 (= 6 hanks)
Red	7544	2
Orange	7606	3
Yellow	7785	4
Green	7344	5
Blue	7319	6
Indigo	7299	7
Violet	7245	4

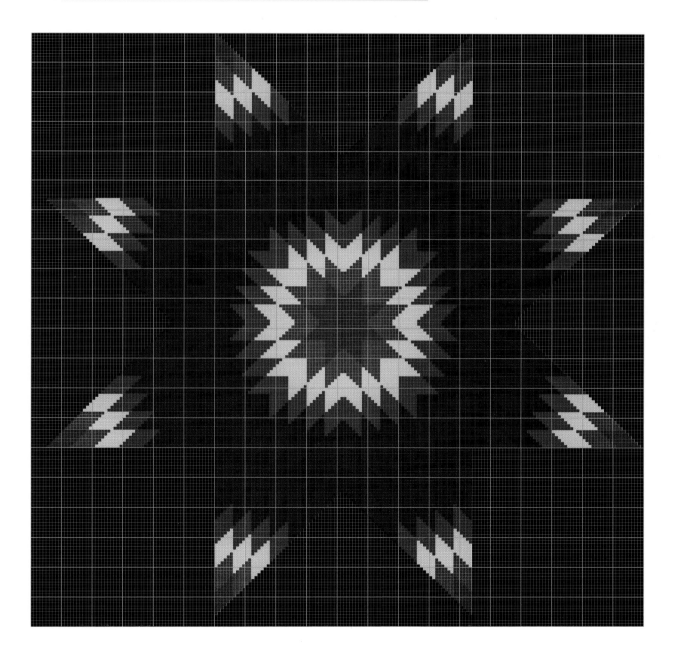

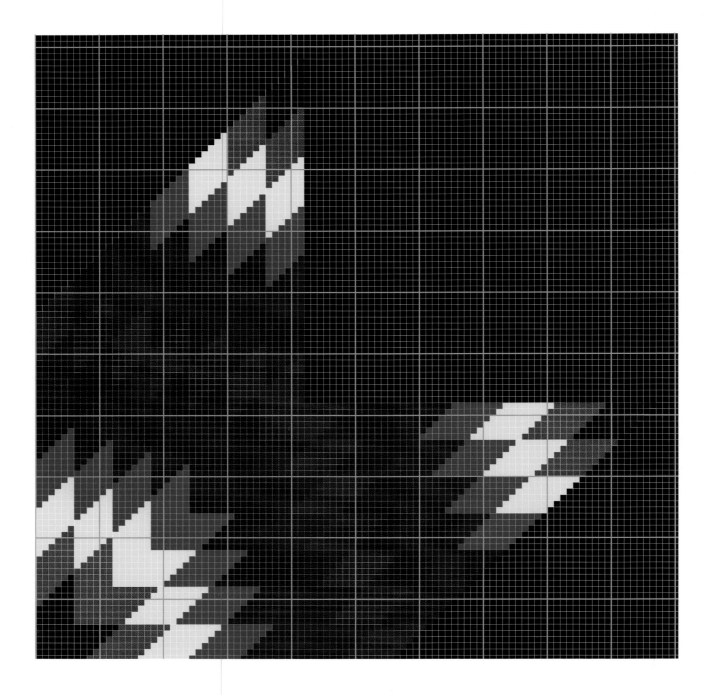

Sunburst
Variation
Pincushion

This striking variant of the Star of Bethlehem design has no large areas of background colour.

Method

As for Rainbow Star of Bethlehem (page 68).

Make up the pincushion following the instructions for a plain cushion on page 109.

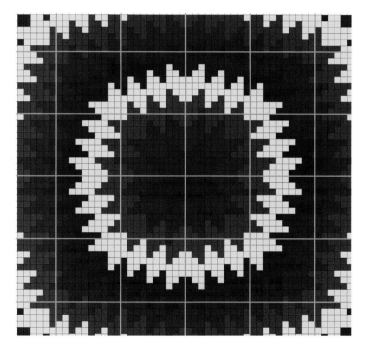

Materials	9½ x 9½in (24 x 24cm) 10-gauge canvas		
	DMC tapestry wool in the following colours and quantities:		
	Colour	No	Skeins
	Dark red	7198	1
	Red	7544	2
	Orange	7606	2
	Yellow	7785	1

Adirondack
Star
Card

Most of the designs in this collection use blocks which are 'butted' together. This means that the blocks are placed directly side by side. This project shows the effect of another common patchwork construction technique called 'sashing', which puts borders between the blocks.

The use of a variegated thread for the sashes and for the central diamonds of each block, along with metallic gold thread at the corners, adds extra sparkle to this card.

Method

The squares shown as pale yellow on the chart represent the areas stitched in two strands of metallic gold.

The orange diamonds at the centre of each block should be stitched using the diagonal basketweave method (see page 105); when using variegated thread, this is more effective than either of the methods which form horizontal rows.

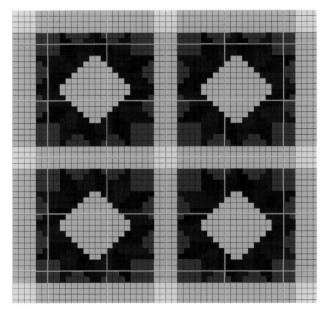

6 x 6in (15 x 15cm) 18-gauge canvas		
DMC coton perlé no. 5 in the following colours (1 skein of each):		
	Colour	**No**
	Green	904
	Bright red	321
	Dark red	815
	Variegated orange	51
DMC stranded cotton (1 skein):		
	Metallic gold	

Materials

Mixed Star Block Sampler
Christmas bellpull

The four star blocks in this project are (from top to bottom): Canadian Star, Patch Star, Another Star, and Farmer's Daughter.

Method

Stitch the blocks from top to bottom. When finished, work five rows of gold at the bottom, and five rows of bronze at the top (these are not shown on the chart), which will be used to wrap around the bellpull ends.

Variations

This design would make a great guitar strap. You could add your own selection of star blocks, or repeat these in a different colour combination, to increase the design to the required length.

7½ x 17½in (19 x 44.5cm) 12-gauge canvas			
DMC tapestry wool in the following colours and quantities:			
	Colour	No	Skeins
	Berry red	7666	1
	Holly green	7429	3
	Bright gold	7056	3
	Bronze	7445	2
	Chestnut brown	7448	2
	Green	7393	1

Materials

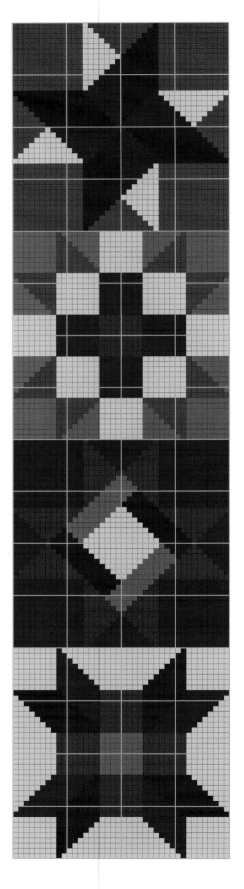

9 Paper Fold Blocks

Life in the early frontier settlements was an isolated affair, offering few opportunities for socializing. Most families were kept busy on their own property, and the nearest neighbour was likely to be an hour or more away on horseback.

When the weather closed in for the winter, even the habitual journeys to church may have been impossible for weeks on end. In New England, 1816 was an exceptionally harsh year, when snow fell and temperatures dropped below freezing in every month of the year. Generations later, it is still known today as 'Eighteen hundred and froze to death'.

Despite this, however, community spirit appears to have been strong, and whenever a job arose requiring communal effort, everyone would pitch in to help their friends – more often than not using it as a good excuse for a party.

These gatherings, known as 'bees', were for activities such as barn raising, corn husking, harvest, and wool carding, and were not purely social events. Every member of every family would have been fully occupied from dawn until dusk.

The exception to this was a 'quilting' or 'quilting bee', which took place when a woman invited her friends to come and help her to assemble and finish the quilt tops which she had stitched during the previous months.

Girls were taught to sew from the age of about four or five, and by the time she reached marriageable age a young woman was expected to have completed a dozen quilt tops for her 'hope chest'. A quilting bee often doubled as an engagement party. As many as six or seven quilt tops could be finished, and the friends of the bride-to-be would plan and make the quilt which would later adorn her wedding bed.

Quilts were also made as gifts for young single men to mark their 21st birthday. These were called 'freedom quilts'.

The projects in this chapter are thought to have been designed by a method which became popular when paper started to be widely available. A square of paper was folded several times then opened out, and the folds were used as a guide to the pattern pieces.

Handy
Andy
Cushion

This cushion was made with a specific location in mind: the battered brown leather fireside chair in a friend's study/den.

I stitched it in the early autumn sun of the south of France, whilst staying with friends. There was some debate at the time about the colours being too strong and harsh, but back in England in winter firelight, they are very cosy indeed.

Method

Start stitching with the terracotta square in the centre of the design, and work each block separately. When all nine blocks are complete, work a border: 4 rows gold, 4 rows terracotta, and 4 rows blue.

Variations

For a slightly different overall effect, use the charted block in the centre and four corners, and reverse the blue and terracotta patches around the edges of the other four (see lower chart on page 78).

Alternatively, as with all the designs in the book, photocopy the Handy Andy grid on page 142 and experiment with your own colour combinations.

Materials

Single block
5 x 5in (12.5 x 12.5cm) 12-gauge canvas
Key square (see page 115) = 12 x 12

	DMC tapestry wool in the following colours and quantities:		
	Colour	**No**	**Skeins**
	Terracotta	7920	2
	Navy blue	7307	2
	Gold	7505	1
	Dark brown	7469	1

Whole cushion front
21 x 21in (53.5 x 53.5cm) 12-gauge canvas

	DMC tapestry wool in the following colours and quantities:		
	Colour	**No**	**Hanks**
	Terracotta	7920	3
	Navy blue	7307	4
	Gold	7505	2
	Dark brown	7469	1

NB: If your stockist does not have hanks of wool, they will be able to advise you on the number of skeins you need to complete the project.

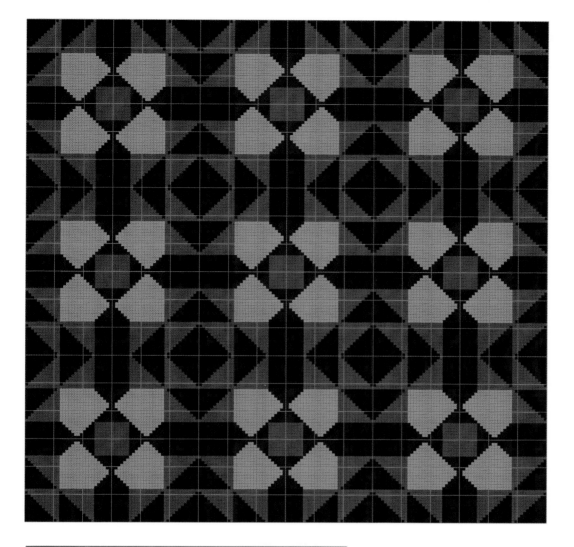

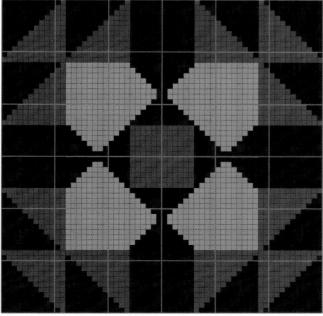

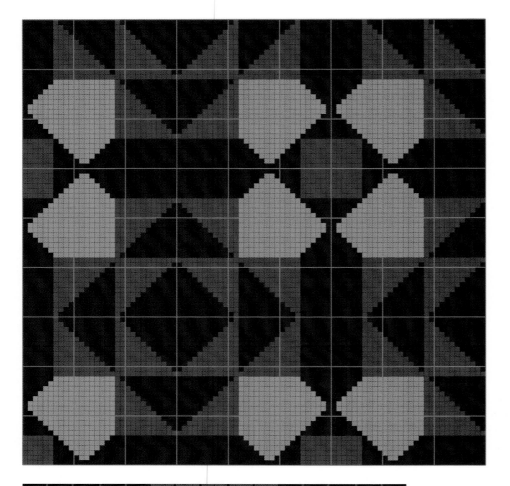

Alternative colour scheme

19½ x 19½in (49.5 x 49.5cm) 12-gauge canvas
Key square (see page 115) = 6 x 6

DMC tapestry wool in the following colours and quantities:

Colour		No	Skeins
	Burgundy	7139	10
	Dark green	7329	13
	White	Blanc	8
	Rose	7196	9
	Grey-green	7692	9

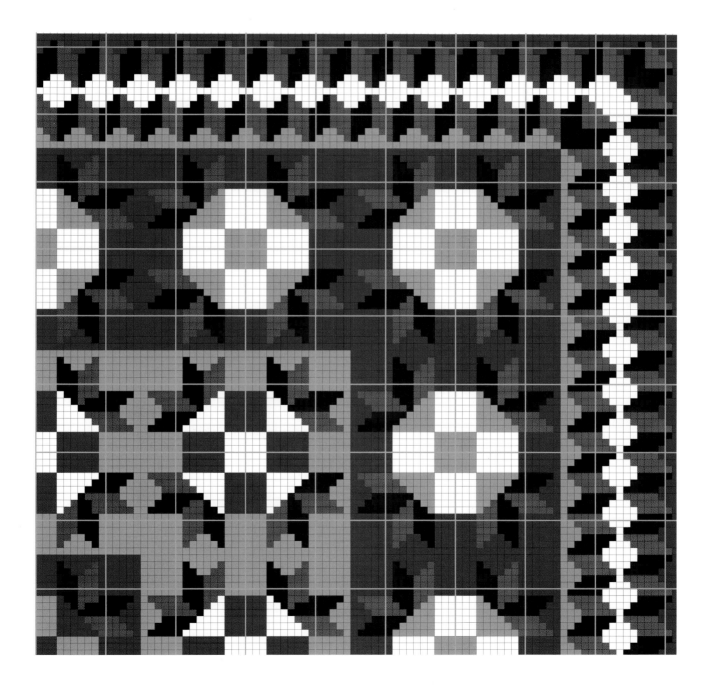

Arrowhead
Cushion

This is a really zingy cushion! A lot is written about colour combinations and designing with a colour wheel to find complementary and contrasting colours, but my only real piece of advice is to experiment; don't be afraid to follow your own instincts.

The brilliant colours used here, contrasted with cream and brown, and the effect of a diagonal lattice superimposed over a square grid, give this design a huge amount of movement. The two outer borders are known as Flying Geese and Chinese Coins.

Method

Use the chart of the single block for each of the nine blocks in the central part of the cushion, and the whole cushion chart for the placement of the border.

Materials

Single block
4 x 4in (10 x 10cm) 12-gauge canvas
Key square (see page 115) = 6 x 6

DMC tapestry wool in the following colours and quantities:		
Colour	**No**	**Skeins**
Cream	7579	2
Red	7544	1
Orange	7947	1
Royal blue	7796	1
Brown	7469	1
Dark green	7389	1

Whole cushion panel
22 x 22in (56 x 56cm) 12-gauge canvas

DMC tapestry wool in the following colours and quantities:		
Colour	**No**	**Skeins**
Cream	7579	13
Red	7544	13
Orange	7947	9
Royal blue	7796	6
Brown	7469	10
Dark green	7389	10

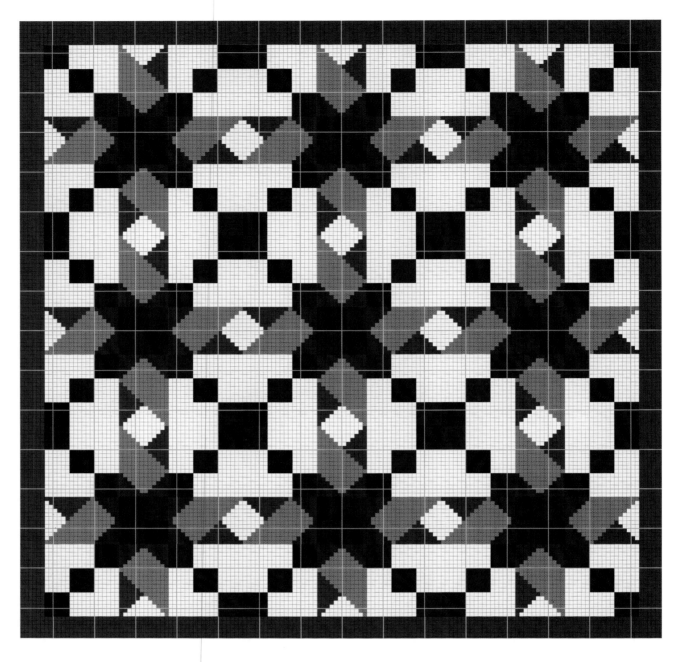

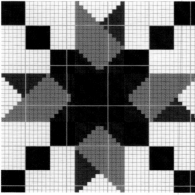

Arrowhead
Variation
Card

This is a quieter version of the
Arrowhead block, which makes
the arrowheads look more like
tulips.

Method

Begin stitching with the two blue
and two blue-green squares in
the centre of the design, and
then stitch the silver star using
two strands of thread.

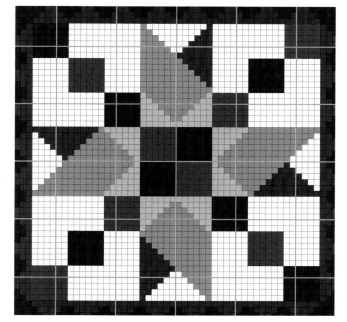

Materials	6 x 6in (15 x 15cm) 18-gauge canvas		
	DMC threads in the following colours (1 skein of each):		
	Colour	No	
	Coton perlé no. 5:		
	Royal blue	796	
	Blue-green	312	
	Dark red	815	
	Pink	335	
	White	Blanc	
	Stranded cotton:		
	Metallic silver		

10 Miscellaneous Patterns

A girl's bridal quilt would have been the first she owned that was appliquéd with hearts, lover's knots, interlocking rings, and other romantic symbols, taken from European folk art. To use such motifs before she was safely engaged was considered to be bad luck – or at the very least, pushing it!

Other superstitions were attached to block names. There is a block called Turkey Tracks, whose original name was Wandering Foot, and it was said that you should never let your children sleep beneath a quilt containing that pattern, because they would grow up to be unhappy or wayward.

From the middle of the eighteenth century, when copperplate printing was developed for the textile industry, appliquéd masterpiece quilts became fashionable. These often took the form of medallion or album quilts.

Medallion quilts are formed of a central panel – sometimes pieced, but often printed – surrounded by a series of borders until the required size is achieved. The designs in this chapter show both forms of medallion; others can be found in the Flora and Fauna chapter.

Album quilts – including the gloriously beautiful Baltimore Brides quilts, many of which have survived – are block quilts where each block is different, in colour or design. Appliquéd album quilts are usually made up of plain squares of fabric, each appliquéd with an individually copperplate-printed motif. Predominant colours were red and green on white or cream, and although flowers and fruit are the most common motifs, I have seen things as bizarre as camels and elephants.

If the album quilt was made by a group of people, each block was often signed and dated. This is particularly true of quilts which were given to mark a special occasion, which, apart from weddings, could be birthdays, anniversaries, or perhaps the departure of a friend or local dignitary, such as a church minister who was moving away from the area.

House on the Hill
Christmas card

There are several house-shaped block designs, the best known being School House, but I think House on the Hill makes a wonderful Christmas card. The snow on the chimneys is added with backstitch.

Method

The approximate midpoint of this design is the bottom left corner of the snowy roof, and you should begin stitching here.

Variations

You could design a version of this block for each season of the year, using different colours, with perhaps the snow giving way to a flower-filled meadow in spring and summer, or a ploughed field in autumn.

The addition of glittery blending filament would add extra sparkle to the snow.

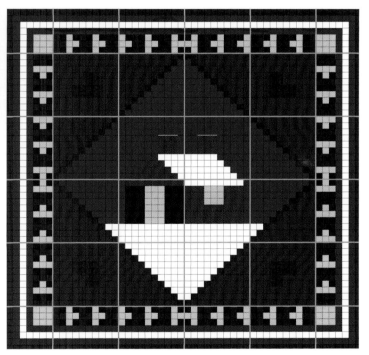

Materials	6 x 6in (15 x 15cm) 18-gauge canvas		
	DMC coton perlé no. 5 in the following colours and quantities:		
	Colour	No	Amount
	Bright red	666	1 skein
	Red	304	1 skein
	Dark grey-blue	930	1 skein
	Gold	972	1 skein
	Dark brown	938	1 skein
	Mid-brown	898	approx. 1yd (1m)
	Red-brown	632	approx. 1yd (1m)
	White	Blanc	1 skein

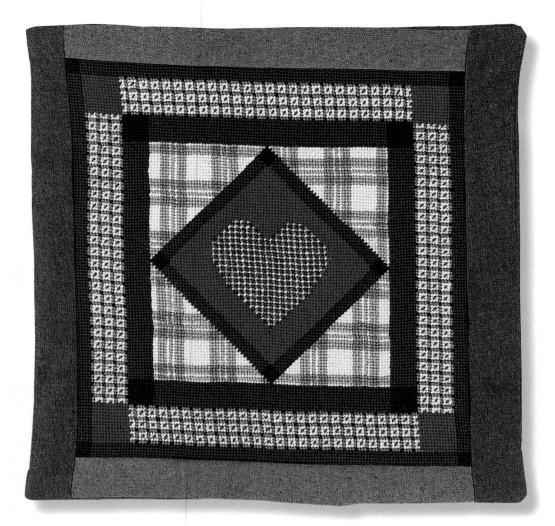

Blue Heart
Photo album cover

The subject of appliquéd quilt designs is too vast to be covered adequately here; this project and the Irish Chain with Flowers are the only two in this collection where the technique would have been used.

Method

The central square has been coloured bright yellow just to help you place the heart correctly. I have not matched the pattern on the blue and white plaid triangles, as I think this adds authenticity, but if the lack of symmetry worries you, you can adjust accordingly.

Variations

To make the heart look as though it has been stitched onto the central diamond, you could add a row of blanket or running stitch around the edge.

15 x15in (38 x 38cm) 12-gauge canvas

DMC tapestry wool in the following colours and quantities:

Colour		No	Skeins
	White	Blanc	6
	Royal blue	7319	8
	Mid-blue	7304	5
	Pale blue	7313	3
	Burnt orange	7360	4
	Very dark navy blue	7308	2

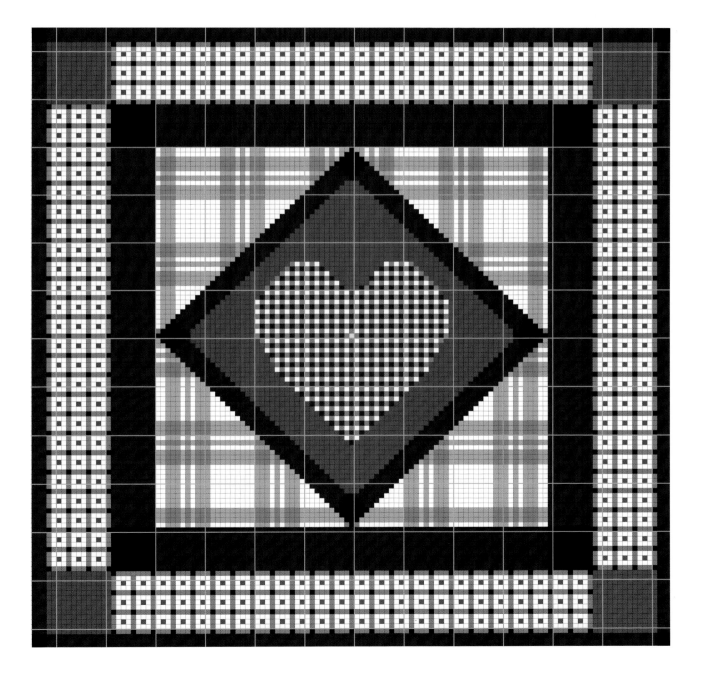

11 Scraps and Oddments

The popularity of quilt making declined in America after the Civil War, when woven blankets were factory made for the first time, and replaced quilts as the main item of household bedding. For all but the poorest families, this meant that patchwork quilting could be looked upon as a leisure activity, rather than a daily chore.

As a result, all sorts of fads and crazes swept both Europe and America. Whole-cloth quilts became popular to show off one's ability to quilt intricate patterns. Many of these were white-on-white designs, and if one lacked either the skill or the time to make one of these very impractical quilts, it was quite common to turn a pieced quilt over and use the white or cream backing as the top. This little deception echoes the habit, in the north of England, of reversing 'strippy' quilts to show the red flannel backing, to give the appearance of a more expensive whole-cloth quilt.

The English court's obsession with mourning after Prince Albert's death in 1861 spread across the Atlantic, manifesting itself in yet further categories of masterpiece quilt: Widows' Quilts, which used mourning colours – black, grey, purple, mauve – or the even more mawkish Memorial Quilts, which were made from remnants of the dear departed's clothing!

It was at this time, also, that the Victorian fad for crazy quilts was born, and although these luscious confections of velvet and embroidered silks were a far cry from the first crazy quilts made from feed sacks and remnants of home-spun, it could be said that trends in American patchwork had come full circle.

Broken Sash
Pillow-sized cushion with covered buttons

The soft, muted shades of terracotta, stone, and old weathered copper could have come straight out of a Mediterranean landscape. In fact, these colours are borrowed from a favourite scarf.

The soft, loose-woven Indian cotton used on front and back was doubled with unbleached calico to give it more substance.

Only a portion of the design is charted here, because, apart from the distribution of dark and light colours, it is completely random.

Follow the instructions on page 111 for covering buttons.

Method

However you choose to arrange the colours, each dark diamond should be surrounded by four pale triangles, and vice versa. This is seen more clearly in the two-colour version on page 95.

Variations

Obviously, as this represents a scrap quilt, you could use any oddments of thread you happen to have left from other projects. If you keep the same balance of dark and light, the effect will be the same.

The chart on page 95 shows the effect of using only two colours.

If you prefer a square cushion rather than this oblong pillow size, you can use any of the other methods of construction outlined on pages 107–10.

This is a design that can be adapted to fit any size or shape, and would be ideal for projects such as drop-in dining-chair seats, or stool tops.

Materials

19 x 19in (48.5 x48.5cm) 12-gauge canvas
Key square (see page 115) = 15 x 15

DMC tapestry wool in the following colours (1 hank (= 5 skeins) of each):

Colour	No		Colour	No
Dark			**Light**	
Brown	7801		Salmon pink	7124
Rust	7447		Mushroom	7520
Green	7377		Beige	7511
Dark blue-green	7288		Pinkish cream	7452
Pale blue-green	7690		Cream	Ecru
Terracotta	7356		Very pale apricot	7171

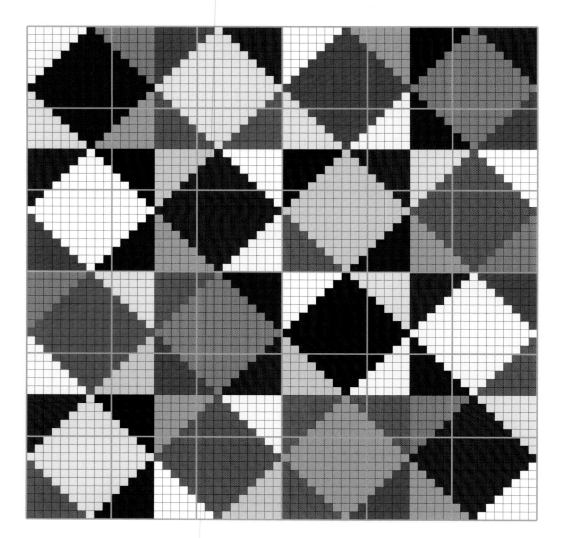

Basket of Scraps
Place mat

This is just one of many 'basket' patterns, and I have also seen it called Grape Basket. I have stayed with a set colour scheme for this place mat, but you could use it to great effect to finish up all your ends of thread.

Method

This design is made from six blocks plus a border; as its centre does not fall at any particularly convenient spot, it is indicated with a cross on the chart. The size of the key square for this design is 10 x 10 stitches.

Variations

By reducing the key square size down to 8 x 8 stitches, one block of this design plus a border would make a coaster to go with this mat.

Materials

14 x 18in (5.5 x 5.5cm) 12-gauge canvas
Key square (see page 115) = 10 x 10

DMC tapestry wool in the following colours and quantities:

Colour		No.	Skeins
	Cream	Ecru	7
	Vary pale apricot	7171	7
	Burnt orange	7360	3
	Brown	7448	2
	Gold	7971	2
	Royal blue	7319	9

Crazy
Box top

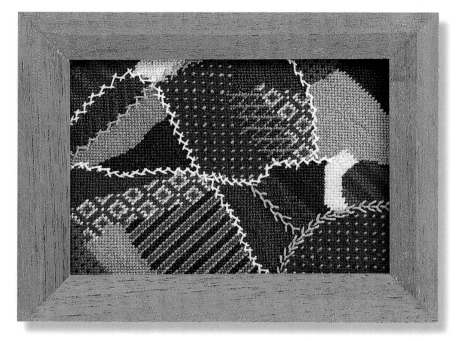

This design is typical of Victorian crazy patchwork in its choice of colour, but is completely random in the size and placement of each 'patch'. Although I have charted the basic stitching, the embellishment would be almost impossible to duplicate exactly, and I would advise you just to 'do your own thing' – use as many different types of thread as you wish, and as much surface embroidery as you feel comfortable with.

At the height of its fashion, the Victorians used this method to cover everything from beds to pianos!

Method

Centre the box top over the canvas and, using a waterproof pen, draw a line around the area to be worked. Begin stitching in the corner of your choice. Don't worry too much about sticking rigidly to the chart – it is only intended as a rough guide. Once the needlepoint is complete, add as much surface stitching (herringbone stitch is traditional) as you wish.

Variations

On a piece this size it would be possible to add beads to your embroidery to add textural interest. On a larger (say cushion-sized) piece, you could add beads, sequins, decorative buttons, or the small metallic charms which are now becoming available from needlework suppliers.

Materials

8½ x 10½in (21.5 x 26.5 cm) 18-gauge canvas

DMC coton perlé no. 5 in the following colours (1 skein of each):

	Colour	No
	Royal blue	791
	Hyacinth blue	797
	Purple	550
	Shocking pink	718
	Red	816
	Warm brown	355
	Mid-brown	898
	Apricot	922
	Gold	783
	Dull gold	729
	Cream	746
	Ecru	Ecru
	Bright green	905
	Dark green	895

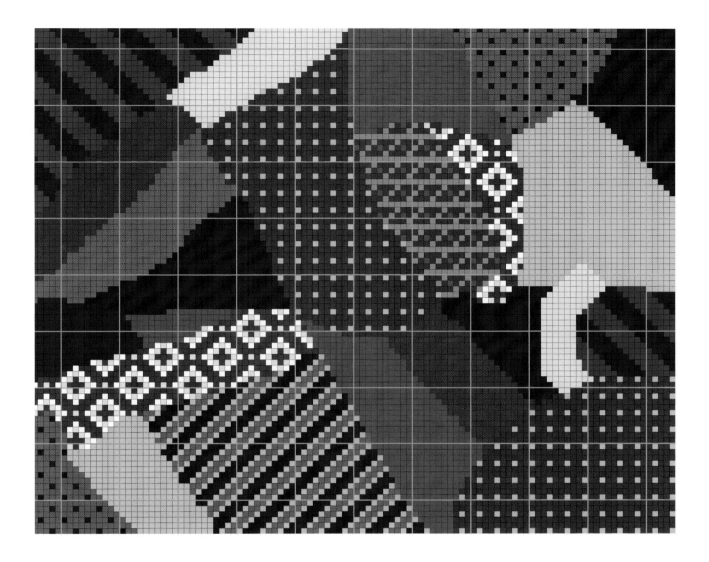

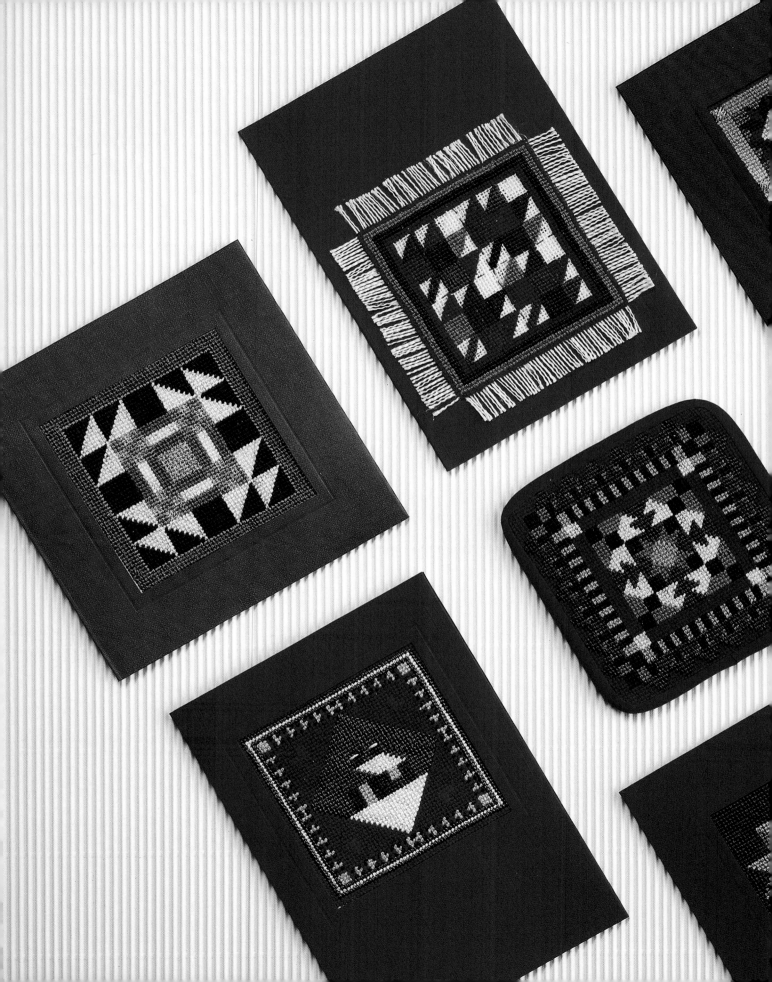

Part Two
How to Do It

12 Materials and Equipment

The list of basic equipment required to start needlepoint is very short and does not need to be expensive. With a few skeins of thread, a piece of canvas, and a packet of needles, you can stitch your first project.

Canvas

Tapestry canvas is usually made of stiffened cotton or linen. There are three main types :

- **Mono** – a single weave.

- **Interlock** – a single weave where the threads are twisted together to form a slightly more rigid base than mono.

- **Double** – also known as **Penelope** – where the weave is formed of pairs of threads.

All come in a variety of widths, and in different gauges, or numbers of threads per inch (2.5cm), and they are available off the roll by the metre, or sometimes in pre-cut pieces. Before buying any canvas you should always check for knots and imperfections, which can ruin the appearance of a project no matter how evenly you stitch.

My personal preference is for single interlock, because it does not fray, and distorts slightly less than the other weaves. With the exception of the Maple Leaf Rug, which is stitched on linen, all the projects in this book have been stitched on 10-, 12-, 14-, or 18-count (or gauge) interlock canvas.

Threads

The projects in this book are stitched in either tapestry wool or coton perlé (the latter either no. 5 or no. 3, depending on the gauge of canvas), with the addition of metallic stranded cotton for some of the cards. When selecting your materials, it is wise to choose a reputable brand, all of which are of consistently high quality with a vast range of colours. Unless you are fortunate enough to live somewhere near a shop which sells more than one brand of thread, you will normally be restricted to using what is available to you locally. This is not necessarily a bad thing, as it can be a blissfully daunting experience to walk into a store which stocks every conceivable make and type of thread.

Purely for the sake of continuity, I have used DMC threads for all these projects, but wherever possible, the Anchor equivalent is given in the conversion charts on page 147.

You should feel free to experiment with your threads. Don't let other people's conventions get in your way. You can stitch successfully on canvas with anything from string to silk ribbon – there are no rules!

Needles

Tapestry needles are blunt, with a long eye to accommodate the thickness of the thread. They are sold in packets of five or six, in single or assorted sizes, and it is always worth buying more than you think you will need, as they become rough and discoloured from the perspiration on your fingers. I am told that it is possible to clean them with fine wire wool or emery paper, but frankly, I'd rather just swap to a new needle and carry on, than waste valuable sewing time. Gold-plated needles cost a little more, but do last longer, so are a good investment.

For 10- and 12-count canvas, you will need a size 18 needle, and for the smaller projects, worked on 18-count canvas, a 24 is the correct size.

Scissors

For a first project, you can probably get away with using any sharp household scissors, but if you decide that needlepoint is for you, then it is worth investing in a small pointed pair to keep exclusively for cutting your threads. The most important thing to bear in mind when buying any pair of scissors is to make sure they fit your fingers and are comfortable to use.

Small scissors have a habit of disappearing down the side of your chair, so you may find it useful to make a small, padded 'scissors keeper' which, when attached by a length of ribbon, will help you to keep track of your favourite pair. The Sunshine and Shadow project is designed to be used for this.

You should use a different pair of scissors for cutting your canvas, as this blunts the blades as quickly as cutting paper. For that very reason, I would not recommend using dressmaking shears – particularly if borrowed – but multi-purpose kitchen scissors, always making sure that they are clean before use.

Frames

Using a frame for your needle-point is entirely a matter of personal preference. If you like

to use one, fine, but don't feel that you have to – the object of the exercise is to be happy and relaxed when you are sewing.

If you like to be able to carry your work with you, so that you can whip it out and be stitching as soon as your bottom hits a convenient seat, you will probably prefer not to use a frame. Canvas is far more forgiving than other kinds of material, and provided you keep your work clean, even if it has been folded or rolled, it will stretch back into shape fairly easily.

If you are a complete beginner, start with a small project, concentrate on trying to get a good even tension to your work, and you will find that a frame is not necessary.

If you do choose to use a frame, you should visit a good needlework shop, to see what is available, and take advice on which sort is best suited to your personal needs.

Masking tape

It is always advisable to bind the edges of your work with masking tape. This helps to prevent the edges fraying, and will also stop the rough edges catching on the threads and – more importantly – your clothes.

Daylight simulation bulbs

Daylight bulbs are widely available for all the standard lamp fittings, whether screw-in or

bayonet. If you cannot work in natural light, then these are very useful, particularly when using certain shades of blue and green, which can look almost identical in normal electric light. The only drawback is that the light they shed is fairly harsh, and can be a little antisocial if you are sharing the room with other people.

13 Needlepoint Techniques

Preparing the canvas

Cut your canvas to the size indicated in the project instructions. This will be the size of the finished article plus 2in (5cm) on all sides for large projects, and a little less on smaller designs, to allow for blocking and stretching when stitching is complete.

Find the centre of the canvas by folding it in half vertically and horizontally, and mark either with a pin, or by lightly drawing a cross with a coloured pencil, the same colour as the thread you will use in that area.

Bind the edges of the canvas with masking tape to prevent it from catching on threads or clothing. You should not underestimate the shredding power of new canvas! It is very unwise to wear your favourite sweater or T-shirt when stitching.

Mount your canvas on a frame, according to the frame manufacturer's instructions, if you prefer to work with one.

Starting and finishing threads

To start a new thread, tie a knot in the end of it and pass the needle from the front to the back of the canvas with the knot about 1in (2.5cm) from the first stitch, and the thread passing under the area about to be covered, so that it will be held in place. When the first few stitches have been sewn, the knot can be snipped off.

To finish, simply run your needle through the back of a few stitches to secure the thread, and cut off, trying not leave a 'tail'.

Stitches

The stitch most people recognize as needlepoint or tapestry stitch is just one of a huge range of canvas embroidery stitches, and, in fact, there are three distinct ways of working it:

Half-cross stitch

This leaves a simple vertical stitch on the reverse of the work, does not cover the canvas terribly well, and is not particu-

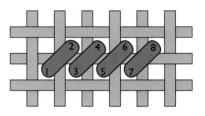

Fig 13.1 Half-cross stitch

larly hard-wearing. For the projects in this book, I would only recommend that you use this variation on cards, or on heavily 'patterned' areas where several colours are used close together.

Tent stitch

The second version of the tapestry stitch covers the canvas well and is fairly hard-wearing, but because it has such a long diagonal on the back of the work, it distorts the canvas quite badly, and even on a small project you will need to stretch and block before finishing (see page 106).

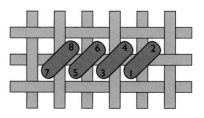

Fig 13.2 Tent stitch

Basketweave stitch

Named because of the appearance of the back of the canvas, basketweave is wonderful for covering large areas. Stitched diagonally from the top right-hand corner of the area to be covered, it produces minimal distortion, and is extremely hard-wearing. I use it for all but the very smallest blocks of colour.

Fig 13.3 Basketweave stitch

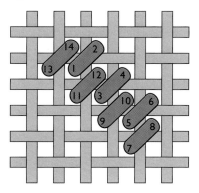

Other stitches

The other stitches shown here have been used to lend textural interest to the Irish Chain projects, and the Crazy Patchwork box top.

Fig 13.4 Rice stitch

Fig 13.5 Triple rice stitch

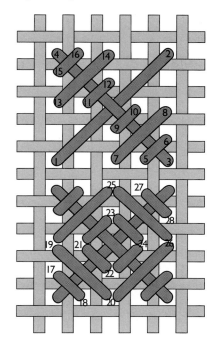

Fig 13.6 Long-legged cross stitch

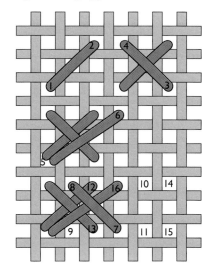

Fig 13.7 Herringbone stitch

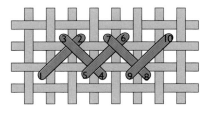

Stitching the projects

You should normally begin stitching in the centre of the design, as this helps to lessen distortion of the canvas.

The best length of thread to use is about 15in (38cm). Any longer than that, and you will find that being pulled through the canvas will cause the yarn to fray and stretch, and your stitches will not give even coverage. For some reason, this is particularly true of some dark colours, which do not cover as well as others.

If your thread becomes twisted, let the needle dangle for a few seconds to unwind before continuing. Do not try to continue stitching; you will only cause knots to form, which can be very frustrating.

14 Finishing your Work

Stretching and blocking

Once your project is stitched, you will almost certainly find that it has distorted into a diamond shape. This is perfectly normal, and will occur even if you use a frame and have the most perfect stitching tension. Pulling your work back into shape is time-consuming, but not difficult, and well worth doing because it can transform the most mediocre piece of stitching into something spectacular.

Many needlework shops offer a stretching service, and some will also arrange to have your work framed if you wish, but if you want to try it yourself, you will need the following equipment:

- a large piece of thick hardboard or MDF;
- a large piece of blotting paper;
- a waterproof pen;
- a rule (preferably metal);
- a right-angle set square;
- a hammer and tacks (preferably rustproof);
- pincers, for removing the tacks;
- a plastic spray bottle and large sponge.

Method

To stretch your work back into shape, place the blotting paper on your board and, using your rule and set square, draw out the exact desired size of the stitched area. Mark the centre of each side.

Place your work, face down, on the paper, and spray lightly and evenly with water. Pat gently with the sponge to make sure that the water penetrates the surface of the stitching. The object of this is to soften the glue which stiffens the canvas, so that when stretched, it will dry back into shape.

Now, using your line as a guide, and matching the corners and centre points of each side, fasten the damp canvas onto the board by hammering tacks around the edge, about ½in (1.25cm) outside the stitching line, and about ½ to 1in (1.25–2.5 cm) apart, depending on how badly distorted it is.

Once you are happy that your work is square, it must be left to dry completely. It is best to leave this to happen naturally, and this can take several days. You may be tempted to lean the board against a radiator, or speed things along by using a hair dryer, but if your work does not dry evenly, further distortion may occur, and you will have to start the stretching process all over again.

Once dry, carefully remove the tacks and check that your work is satisfactorily squared. If not, you can repeat the stretching process as many times as required. You should read the instructions for making up your project before trimming away any of the spare canvas.

Taking care of your work

It is not possible to wash needle-point, and cleaning must be limited to shaking cushions and gently vacuuming upholstered pieces, so at this point you should give some thought to the amount of wear that your finished piece will be subjected to. It may be worth treating it with a 'spill-proofing' spray; these are widely available from craft, haberdashery, and shoe shops. If your work does become soiled, you must take it to be professionally cleaned.

You should always try to avoid pressing the stitched area of your work, as this will flatten the surface. If it does become necessary, then you should place at least three thick, fluffy layers of towelling under the work, which should be face down, and a clean, damp cloth over it.

Pictures

The Ohio Star project is specifically designed to fit into a shop-bought frame: 8 x 10in (20.5 x 25.5cm) with a ready-cut mount, or 6 x 8in (15 x 20.5cm) without one. These are standard sizes for ready-made frames, and are available in a wide range of colours and styles. The instructions given here are for mounting a picture of this sort of size.

If you are thinking of framing anything larger, such as the Pineapple Log Cabin panel, you will have to take your work to a professional framer. It is worth finding one in your area who will also stretch your work, but if you choose to do this yourself, you should not trim the canvas away afterwards, because there are things like mounts and frame apertures to take into consideration.

Always make sure you check your work for missed or misplaced stitches before you hand it over to be framed; when stretched and mounted, your mistakes will leap up and hit you in the eye, and by then it will be too late to put them right.

If you want to have glass put in your frame, you should discuss this with your framer, as it may govern your choice of frame moulding. I never have glass in mine, as I think it deadens the colours, and it nearly always squashes the stitching.

Lacing your work for framing

Using the backing board from your frame as a guide, cut a piece of acid-free mount board (thick card available from art shops) to the same size, minus approximately ⅛in (3mm) on all sides to allow for the thickness of the canvas. Mark the centre of each side of the board. Centre the canvas over the board, making sure that the design will be in the right place to show through the mount, if you are using one.

Push pins through the canvas into the edges of the board, making sure that the grain of the canvas remains straight.

Turn the whole lot over. Fold the corners in diagonally, and hold in place with masking tape. Using a long, strong thread (crochet cotton or thin string are ideal) with a needle at each end, and starting from the middle, lace the top and bottom of the canvas across the back of the board. When you reach the edge, gently take up the slack until taut, and knot the ends securely together. Repeat with the other half, and then repeat the process with the other two sides (see Fig 14.1).

Remove the pins and reassemble the frame, preferably omitting the glass for the reasons given above.

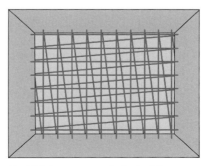

Fig 14.1 Lacing across the back of the canvas

Cushions
(also pincushions, scissors keeper, sachets)

The majority of the projects in this book are cushions, and the method of construction is purely a matter of personal choice.

Backing fabric

When selecting your backing fabric, you should bear in mind that your finished canvas is itself a heavyweight piece of cloth, and if you choose anything lighter than furnishing weight fabric, you may have to reinforce it. This is quite simple to do. The red gingham I used for the patterned version of the Martha Washington Star is very flimsy on its own, so I backed it with calico, to add some bulk, before use. All you have to do is cut out identical pieces, and tack them together. Treated as one layer of fabric, this does not alter the method of construction.

Velvet is the classic choice for backing needlepoint, but it can be quite tricky to handle, and does not always fit into a modern room setting.

Cotton of a medium-weight furnishing quality, available in a huge range of colours, is suitable for most projects, but you should not be afraid to experiment. Stripes, checks, and denims all work well with patchwork designs, as does a softer, more open-weave Indian cotton, which – like the gingham – needs to be lined with calico to give it sufficient strength.

Most important of all, you must make sure that the colour you select complements your needlework rather than detracting from it. If in doubt, choose one of the colours from the design.

I have not specified the quantities of material to be used for backing and borders in the individual project instructions, as I feel that finished size and method of construction should be a matter of personal choice. As a rough guide, however, 0.5 metre of 120cm wide furnishing fabric is more than enough to make up an 18 x 18in (46 x 46cm) square cushion using any of the methods given below.

The cushion front

It is not necessary to add a border to your cushion front, but this does help to reduce the bulk of the seams, and also enables a fairly small piece of needlepoint to be made up into a large project.

Figure 14.2 shows three styles of border: the first two – appropriately in this collection – are taken from Log Cabin patchwork, and the third has classically mitred corners.

Log Cabin border 1

Cut four strips of the required width to the following lengths, plus a ½in (1.25cm) seam allowance on all four sides (see Fig 14.2a):

- Length A = the width of the canvas.
- Length B = the width of the canvas plus the width of strip A.
- Length C = the width of the canvas plus the width of strip B.
- Length D = the width of the canvas plus the width of strip A and strip C.

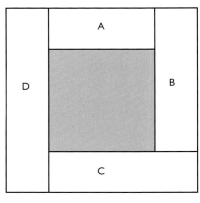

Fig 14.2 Three styles of cushion border

a Log Cabin

b Courthouse Steps

c Mitred

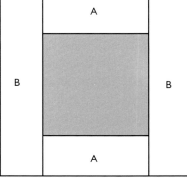

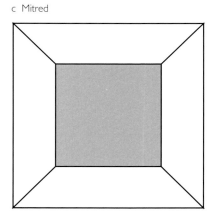

With right sides together, using a sewing machine or hand-sewn back stitch, sew the first strip (A) to the canvas along the edge of the needlepoint. Press the seam towards the border.

Repeat with strips B, C, and D.

Top-stitching the border very close to the edge of the needle-point stabilizes the whole cushion front and makes it lie flatter, but this is optional (see Fig 14.3).

Fig 14.3 Top-stitching the border

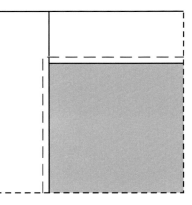

Log Cabin border 2 (Courthouse Steps)

Cut four strips of the required width to the following lengths, plus a ½in (1.25cm) seam allowance on all four sides:

- Length of strips A = the width of the canvas.
- Length of strips B = the width of the canvas plus twice the width of strip A (see Fig 14.2b).

With right sides together, sew the two strips A to opposite sides of the canvas along the edge of the needlepoint. Press the seams towards the border. Repeat with strips B. Again, the border can be top-stitched if desired.

Mitred border

This can be very tricky. Until you are fairly experienced, I would recommend using one of the other methods.

Cut four strips of the required width. The length of all four will be the size of the canvas plus 2 border widths, with ½in (1.25cm) all round as seam allowance (see Fig 14.4).

Fig 14.4 Pieces for mitred border

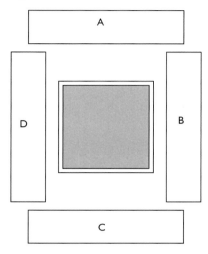

With right sides together, and matching the centre of the long side of strip A to the centre of one side of the canvas, sew along the edge of the needlepoint, stopping at the corner of the stitched area, and *not* running into the seam allowance at either end (Fig 14.5).

Repeat with strip B, taking great care at the corner not to catch any of strip A. Add strips C and D in the same way, so that all four strips are attached to the sides of the canvas, but not to each other.

Now fold each end of each strip at 45° from the corner of the needlepoint, and crease sharply or mark with pins, chalk, or tacking stitches.

Still with right sides together, pin and sew the strips together along these diagonal lines, making sure that the canvas remains free. Trim the corner of the canvas diagonally to reduce bulk, and cut away the superfluous triangles of the border strips to within ½in (1.25cm) of the diagonal seams. Press these seams open. Top-stitch the border if you wish.

The cushion back

Plain back

If you choose to, you can make up your cushion without any opening at all. This is quite suitable if the cushion is not going to be sat upon or leant against, so that all you need to do to keep it reasonably clean is to give it a good shake now and then. This is also the method to use for ring pillows and pincushions, apart from those mounted on a wooden base.

Cut out the backing material to the same dimensions as the cushion front, including the border, if you have added one.

With right sides together, stitch the two layers along three sides, pivoting at the corners. On the fourth side, leave a gap in the middle large enough to squash your cushion pad through, without putting too much strain on the stitching. (Feather-filled pads are best for this, because you can move the filling about; pincushions can be stuffed with any available oddments.)

Carefully trim diagonally across the corners to reduce bulk, and turn right sides out.

Using something blunt like the wrong end of a pencil, push the corners out, taking great care not to poke the trimmed canvas through the stitching from inside. You will not get a very sharp corner, so don't try!

Place the cushion pad in the cover. Turn under the remaining seam allowances and close the gap using slip-stitch.

Zips

If you wish to insert a zip in the back of your cushion, you will need two pieces of fabric, each measuring just over half the width of the cushion front. As an example: where the front of the cushion measures 16in (40.5cm) square, including seam allowances, the two pieces for the back should each measure 16 x 9in (40.5 x 23cm).

Place the two pieces right sides together, and stitch the central seam (one of the long sides) for a short distance at each end, leaving space for the zip. Insert the zip following the manufacturer's instructions. Open the zip enough to get your hand through

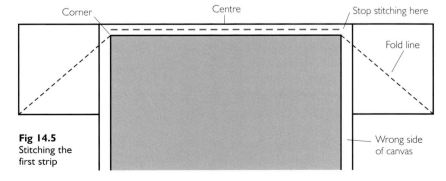

Corner   Centre   Stop stitching here

Fold line

Fig 14.5
Stitching the first strip

Wrong side of canvas

the gap, then, with right sides together, sew the cushion front to the back around all sides, pivoting at the corners.

Trim the corners diagonally. Open the zip and turn the cushion right side out.

Pillowcase opening (housewife)

If you do not wish to use a zip, but feel you will need to replace the cushion pad from time to time, or at least remove it for cleaning, you can make an opening at one end of the cushion with overlapping flaps, like that in a pillowcase.

To do this, you will need to cut a piece of fabric the same size as the front of the cushion, plus about 2in (5cm) to turn under and neaten on one edge, and a second piece, 6in (15cm) wide, which will form a flap (A) to hold the pad in place (see Fig 14.6).

With right sides together, stitch flap A to the cushion front B, down one long side. Leave flap A folded out. Neaten the edge of the strip's other long side by turning under ½in (1.25cm), pressing, and top-stitching about ¼in (6mm) from the edge.

With right sides together, stitch the backing piece C to the cushion front B down the opposite long

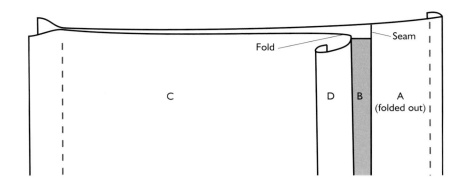

Fig 14.7 Assembling the pillowcase cushion

side, stopping at the corners.

Match and pin the seams at top and bottom of piece C, but do not stitch. Make a double fold on the free side of C, so that the outside edge of the second fold exactly meets the seam where A and B meet (Fig 14.7).

Press the folds and top-stitch ¼in (6mm) from the edge, and

Fig 14.8 The cushion complete and ready to be turned right side out

again at ¾in (2cm), so that quite a firm edge is created.

Now stitch the top and bottom seams, ending at the seam between A and B.

Fold flap A over piece C, and stitch the short seams from D to E (Fig 14.8).

Trim the corners diagonally, and turn right sides out.

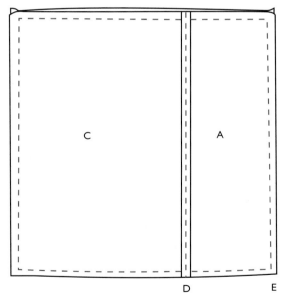

Fig 14.6 Materials for cushion with pillow-case opening

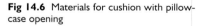

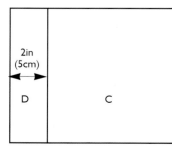

This arrangement should hold your pad in place quite securely, as long as it is not too fat, but you may, if you wish, add tie fastenings, decorative buttons, Velcro, or poppers to close the opening.

Rectangular cushions

To make a rectangular pillow-sized cushion, as shown in the Broken Sash project (page 93), stretch and block your work in the usual way and trim the raw canvas to within ½in (1.25cm) of the stitched area. Now cut a piece of furnishing fabric the same depth as your canvas and half the width.

With right sides together, sew this to side of the canvas and open out to form an oblong. This then becomes the pillow front, and can be made up in any of the ways outlined above. My version of the Broken Sash uses the 'housewife' zipless method of construction, with the opening fastened by three large buttons covered with needlepoint.

Covered buttons

Large buttons designed to be covered with fabric are available from any good haberdashery department; these come with a guide to the size of the material required to cover each button. To cover them in 18-count canvas, you should be able to follow the manufacturer's instructions without a problem. With 10- or 12-count canvas, however, you will not be able to use the snap-on back, or the little teeth designed to grip the fabric. The solution is to lace the canvas onto the buttons, like a tiny pin-cushion (see page 107), and then glue on a circle of felt with a slit cut in the centre to accommo-date the shank of the button.

Coasters and place mats

Any needlepoint which is to be used as a place mat or coaster should be treated before use with one of the spill-resistant sprays which are readily available for carpets and upholstery.

Coasters

Coasters can be mounted in one of the clear plastic coasters that are now available in good needlework shops, or by mail order from various suppliers. You should bear in mind, however, that these are designed primarily for use with thin fabric worked with cross stitch, not canvas and wool.

Small photo frames are also sometimes suitable to use as coaster mounts, but I would recommend replacing the glass with unbreakable plastic, or removing it entirely.

Alternatively, you can work a row of long-legged cross stitch around the border of your stitch-ing, which helps to give a firm plaited edge, and then lace the canvas over a piece of card, as you would for a picture (see page 107).

Finally, for a soft finish, trim the spare canvas to within a couple of threads and stick or tack the coaster to a piece of felt. Trim this to the same size as the canvas, and cover the edges with bias binding.

Place mats

Place mats, like coasters, can be stretched over card and backed with felt, or edged with bias binding; but they can also be constructed like a cushion - plain or bordered – omitting the pad. If you use the 'housewife' flap method, you could slip a piece of card or cork inside, for an extra layer of stiffness or insulation.

Footstools and wooden pincushions

Footstools and ornamental pin-cushions come pre-upholstered and covered in calico, and sit on their base or legs, secured from underneath by a screw. They do not come in any standard size, so to cover them with your needle-point you will probably need to adapt the design to fit, by adjust-ing the amount of background, or width of border. You should always start with a larger piece of canvas than you think you will need, because no matter how carefully you measure the upholstered pad, it will always turn out to be bigger than you think, and you may need to add a few more rows of stitches at the end to prevent the canvas from showing. I speak from bitter experience on this, so humour me, and add a couple of inches.

For a round object, your finished stitching will need to be roughly octagonal rather than square. To do this, you simply leave out the corners of a square design (see Fig 14.9). The amount to be omitted will depend on the size and curvature of the pad, so you should stitch the centre of the design and work out towards the corners,

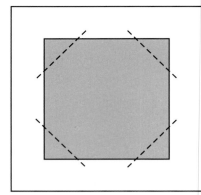

Fig 14.9 Adapting a square design to an octagon

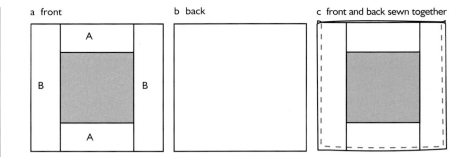

Fig 14.10 Materials for tote bag

Bags

To make a tote bag front from a small piece of needlepoint, you will need to mount your work in a border in the same way as for a cushion front (see pages 108–9). For a larger piece like the Rainbow Star of Bethlehem, you will not need to mount it, but you will need to add a band of your chosen fabric along the top edge which is at least 2in (5cm) deep. Cut another piece of fabric the same size to form the back of the bag, and with right sides together, sew up three sides (Fig 14.10).

Depending on what you are intending to use it for, you may

trying it over the pad as you approach the edges, until the stitched area is large enough.

Once you are happy that your stitching will fit, block it in the usual way. Trim the excess canvas to leave 2in (5cm) on a large project, or 1in (2.5cm) on a small one. Centre the canvas over the padding, and lace tightly across the back, in much the same way as a picture (see page 107), but paying particular attention to the corners, which should be tight and smooth, not loose or creased.

wish to add another couple of rows of stitching to make the seam stronger. Then turn right sides out.

Repeat the exercise with two pieces of lining fabric. Leave this lining bag with seams to the outside, and place inside the canvas bag with seams and raw edges matching. Tack or pin the top edges together.

Make handles by cutting two pieces of strong fabric, 3in (7.5cm) wide and as long as you think you will want them – either short handles, or long shoulder-length straps. Experiment with strips of paper until you get the length right for you, then add 4in (10cm).

Fold in ½in (1.25cm) on each long side, then fold the strips in half lengthways, so that they are 1in (2.5cm) wide. Press and stitch close to the open side, then top-stitch the folded side to match.

Place these on the outside of the bag, so that the ends project

upwards for 2in (5cm), and each end is about 4in (10cm) from the centre. Baste in place (Fig 14.11).

Measure the distance between the side seams of the bag, and cut a single strip of cloth to form the top facing, twice that length plus 1in (2.5cm), and the same depth as the border strip at the top of the bag. Join the two short edges, and press the seam open. Press under ½in (1.25cm) on one long side.

Now, matching right sides and raw edges, sew the facing around the top of the bag, trapping the handle ends between the two layers. Turn the facing strip to the inside of the bag, and sew the bottom edge in place. Top-stitch around the top edge close to the edge, and again about ¼in (6mm) lower. Strengthen the handles by stitching through the 2in (5cm) strip which is now sandwiched inside the top of the bag (Fig 14.12).

Fig 14.11 Positioning the handle

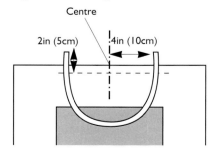

Centre

2in (5cm)   4in (10cm)

Fig 14.12 Stitching through handle and facing strip

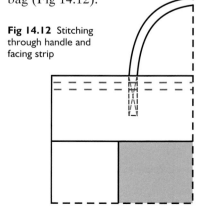

Album covers

Make up the front like a cushion front, with your choice of border. The dimensions should be those of the album front plus 1in (2.5cm) on all sides.

Cut another piece of fabric to the same size for the back cover, and join the two together down one side. Press the seam open.

Cut two pieces of fabric for the end flaps, at least 5in (12.5cm) wide and the same height as the front and back (Fig 14.13). Turn under and stitch ½in (1.25cm) on one long side of each of these two pieces.

With right sides together, sew one of these flaps to the front of the cover, taking up the 1in (2.5cm) seam allowance (Fig 14.14).

Keeping the cover wrong side out, slip it onto the album and pin the second flap in place, making sure that when the album in closed there is still about ½in (1.25cm) ease, to allow for the album's expansion when full of photographs.

Sew the second flap into place, trim the corners diagonally, and turn the whole cover right sides out.

Turn the remaining raw edge under and stitch, taking care not to catch the flaps (Fig 14.15).

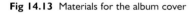

Fig 14.13 Materials for the album cover

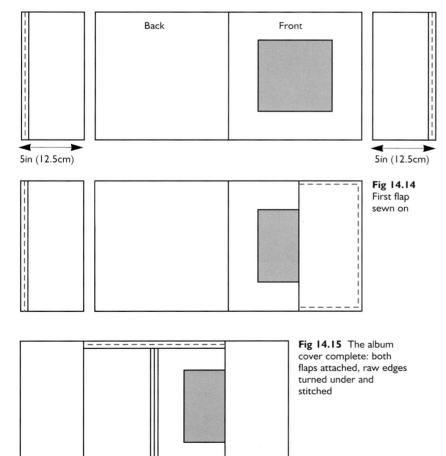

5in (12.5cm)   5in (12.5cm)

Fig 14.14 First flap sewn on

Fig 14.15 The album cover complete: both flaps attached, raw edges turned under and stitched

Curtain tiebacks

To make up the Fence Rail project you will need the following materials:

- 5 x 24in (12.5 x 61cm) backing fabric
- 5 x 24in (12.5 x 61cm) heavyweight iron-on Vilene
- Sewing thread to match
- 2 x D-shaped brass rings
- Approximately 2yd (2m) of purchased cord to trim (optional)

Stretch and block the needlepoint as normal, then trim the excess canvas to about ½in (1.25cm). Turn under the edges and press, making sure that you have lots of squashy towels under the stitched area to prevent it being crushed.

Cut a piece of heavyweight iron-on Vilene to a size just a fraction smaller than the tieback, and iron it onto the wrong side of your chosen lining fabric, which should be the same size as the stitched area plus ½in (1.25cm) seam allowance on all sides. Turn the edges of the lining to the back, and press. Place the lining on the back of the tieback, tack in place, and slip-stitch. Add a length of decorative cord all the way round if you wish.

Finally, sew a brass ring securely to the centre of each short side.

Box tops

Cut a piece of card to the size of the aperture in the lid.

Cut a piece of 4oz wadding to the same dimensions.

Centre the canvas over the card, and lace in the same way as a picture (see page 107). Mount into the box lid following the manufacturer's instructions. Glue a piece of felt to the back if you wish.

For the two little Log Cabin boxes, you could use cotton wool instead of wadding.

Bellpulls

For information on where to obtain the bellpull ends, see Stockists on page 150.

Trim the spare canvas to about ½in (1.25cm) after stretching and blocking. Fold this to the back of the canvas on the long sides and press, making sure you have enough padding under the stitching to prevent it being squashed.

Position the canvas through the bellpull ends, and fold down onto the back. Sew securely in place. Cut a piece of felt to fit the back of the bellpull and either glue or slip-stitch in place.

Spectacle cases

Cut a piece of felt or other soft fabric to the same size as the stitched area, plus a seam allowance of no more than ¼in (6mm).

Fold all the spare canvas to the back of the stitched area, and baste to hold in place.

Trim the spare canvas to about ½in (1.25cm). Fold the resulting square in half and over-sew one long and one short side, using wool to match the pattern when possible.

Remove the basting stitches. Fold the felt in half and sew up one long and one short side. Slide into place inside the canvas, and slip-stitch together at the opening of the glasses case.

Trim with purchased cord if you wish.

Cards

Stick pieces of double-sided sticky tape around the edge of the card aperture (B in Fig 14.16).

Fig 14.16 Ready-made window card with double-sided tape around inside of opening

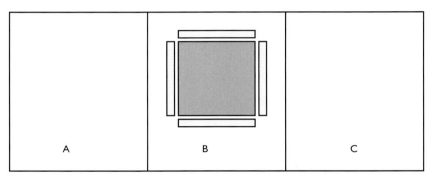

Trim spare canvas to about ½in (1.25cm). Centre your stitching carefully and stick to B with the tape.

Shield the inside of the card (C) with a piece of paper, and spray the back of A and B lightly with spray-mount, being careful to follow the instructions on the can. Fold A onto B and weight down until firmly stuck.

Fig 14.17 Construction of needlecase

If you are nervous about using spray-mount, or other glue, you can stick A to B using double-sided tape.

Needlecases

These will normally consist of two squares of needlepoint, stitched side by side to form a rectangle. I would advise stitching a row of long-legged cross stitch (see page 105) around this, as it forms a natural edging.

Once stretched, trim the spare canvas to within ½in (1.25cm) and turn under. Cut a piece of felt to fit and slip-stitch in place. Cut another rectangle of felt, slightly smaller. Fold this in half to form two squares, and crease down the fold. Open out again and match with the centre of the lining felt. Using back stitch, sew the second piece of felt in place through all layers (Fig 14.17).

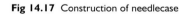

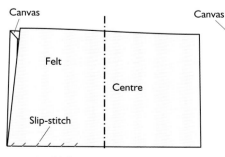

Canvas

Felt

Centre

Slip-stitch

a sewing felt lining to canvas

Canvas

Felt

Felt

b attaching the inner leaves of felt

15 Adapting the Designs

In keeping with their origins, I have tried to make the projects in this book as flexible as possible. You can change the colours and the size of each one. You can make a plain project patterned, or a patterned project plain. You can design and use your own patterns or, with the aid of the grids on pages 125–46, alter the balance of a design by changing the position of dark and light areas.

Changing the size of a design

There are two ways of altering the size of the designs in this book. You can leave the design the same, and use a different gauge of canvas, so that, for example, a block of 12 x 12 stitches which measures 1in (2.5cm) on 12-count canvas becomes around ⅝in (1.6cm) on 18-count canvas, or a little over 1¾in (4.5cm) on 7-count.

The alternative is to change the design itself. The designs in this book, with the exception of the Blue Heart album cover and the two box tops worked in Random Log Cabin and Crazy Patchwork, are all geometric. Each block design has a key

square which, once in place, governs the size and placement of all the other shapes.

To illustrate this, we can look at one of the Paper Fold blocks, Handy Andy (Fig 15.1). The basic block, when broken down into its component parts, is made from 25 squares (5 x 5), some of which are

then subdivided into triangles. If each of these squares is 12 stitches across, then the whole block is 60 stitches across, which on 12-count canvas is 5in (12.5cm).

If you want to adapt the block to fit into a box top which has (say) a 3½in (9cm) aperture, you need to calculate as follows:

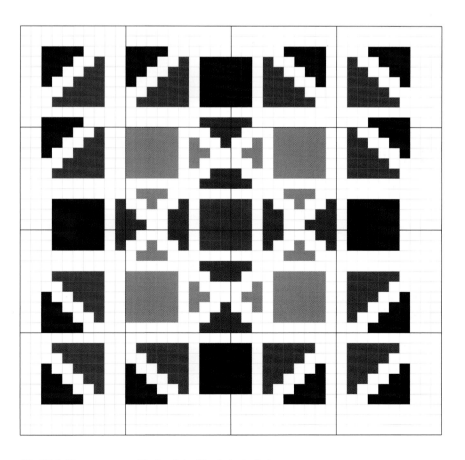

Fig 15.1 The component blocks of the Handy Andy design

- 3½in on 12-count canvas = 42 stitches.
- The block is 5 squares wide. 42 divided by 5 = 8 with 2 left over.

So if you stitch your design using 8 x 8 stitches as the size of your key square, instead of 12 x 12, you will only need to add a border of one row of stitching all round for it to fit your box top perfectly. (You could, of course alter the gauge of canvas at the same time.)

If you wanted to stitch Handy Andy on 18-count canvas to fit a 3in (7.5cm) card aperture, the calculations are as follows:

- 3in on 18-count canvas = 54 stitches.
- 54 divided by 5 = 10 with 4 left over.

So your key square becomes 10 x 10 stitches instead of 12 x 12, and you will need to work two rows of border all round to make the design fit the card.

There are only a couple of things you need to bear in mind when adapting these designs:

- If you start with an even-numbered stitch count in your key square, you cannot change it to an odd number without altering the design slightly. It is better to change even to even or odd to odd.
- There is a minimum size for each shape, which is governed by the number of stitches used. For instance: a square has to have a minimum of 2 x 2 stitches; a square cut into two triangles must be at least 3 x 3 stitches, and there will always be a 'dominant' triangle (Fig 15.2).

Fig 15.2 Some basic shapes reduced to their minimum possible sizes

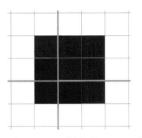

a   a square

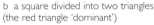

b   a square divided into two triangles (the red triangle 'dominant')

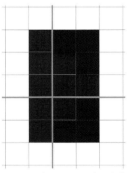

c   a wedge or arrowhead shape

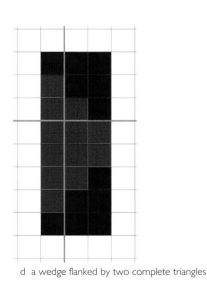

d   a wedge flanked by two complete triangles

Where a project is made up of a series of identical patchwork blocks, I have, wherever possible, charted the single block as well as the whole project, and indicated the size of its key square, so that you can use the block in your own way.

Adding borders

Borders are a very useful way of changing the size of a project, and you will find a small selection of traditional designs on page 122, and others in the charts for the Shady Pines, Dutch Rose, Arrowhead, and Blue Heart projects.

Colour and scale can be changed to suit your own needs, and all these border designs can be mixed with any of the block designs in the book. You could even create a design made entirely from strips of border, or surround a plain coloured square with a series of borders.

There are two ways of tackling corners. The first is to use the 'sashing' method and place a plain square at each corner, as in the Blue Heart project (page 90). The alternative is to work out a way of turning the border design round the corner (as in the Dutch Rose, page 65), which is best done on graph paper. A useful trick to help you with this is to use a small frameless mirror held vertically at 45° across the border on the chart, which will show you the effect of mitring the corner.

Once you are happy with the corners, you need to think about the centre of each side. Do you want the corners to be identical? If so, what happens to the design where the patterns meet? The border design may need to change direction (as in the Arrowhead, page 85), in which case you will need to find a way of handling this, such as placing a plain square or diamond in the centre.

Changing plain to patterned

To change a plain block into a patterned one is quite easy. First of all, you need to decide on a pattern: this can be one of mine, from the selection on pages 123–4, or one of your own. Remember that my patterns are intended as guides only – your colour scheme should be your own choice.

On graph paper, draw out your pattern so that it covers an area twice the size of the largest patch in your chosen block – so that if your largest patch is 12 x 12 stitches square, your pattern should cover at least 24 x 24 squares on the graph paper.

Now, from another piece of graph paper, cut a hole 12 x 12 squares in size, and position it randomly over your design so that a portion of it appears through the hole. This is the equivalent of placing a template on fabric and cutting it out. You don't have to match the pattern where two patches meet. In fact, it will look more authentic if you don't.

If you feel unhappy about designing your own patterns, and don't want to use any of mine, you can use a shop-bought iron-on transfer, or a rubber stamp.

To do this, mask off the surrounding area with paper, and iron the transfer, or press the inked stamp, directly onto your graph paper, where you can then colour it in with coloured pencils.

Even if you are feeling particularly brave, I would not advise putting the design directly on to the canvas, because it is not possible to rectify mistakes. You must also bear in mind that the ink would probably show through pale-coloured thread when stitched.

Blank blocks and grids

On pages 125–46 you will find line diagrams of many of the designs in the book. These are for you to photocopy and colour in to create your own patterns. They can be enlarged on the photocopier to any convenient size.

There are endless possibilities. You will find that you can change the appearance of a design completely, simply by altering the colour of the pattern pieces. This is illustrated by the two designs shown in Fig 15.3 overleaf, which are made up of exactly the same patchwork block (Hands All Round), but coloured in different ways.

Fig 15.3 The same design in two different colour schemes: Hands All Round

What to make?

Here is a list of ideas for things you could make using patchwork blocks in needlepoint.

Squares or rectangles - either single or multiple blocks	
Scissors keeper	Key fob
Gift tag	Box tops
Card	Picture
Coaster	Sachet
Pincushion	Stool top
Patch pocket	Cushion centre
Ring pillow	Bag front panel
Album cover	Bag
Cushion	Mat
Spectacle case	Chequebook cover
Needlecase	

Strips	
Bellpull	Belt
Guitar strap	Tray hanger
Curtain tieback	Shelf edging
Luggage strap	Skirt border
Hatband	Napkin ring

All-over patterns	
Cushion	Chair seat
Stool or bench top	Bag
Waistcoat	

Patterns and Borders

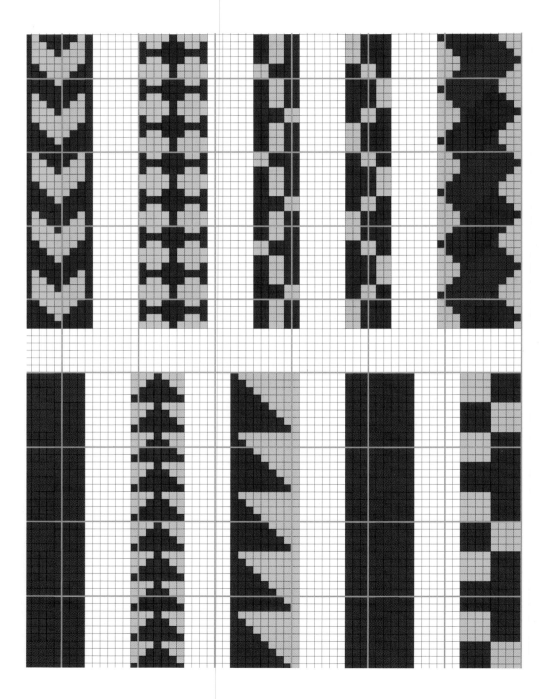

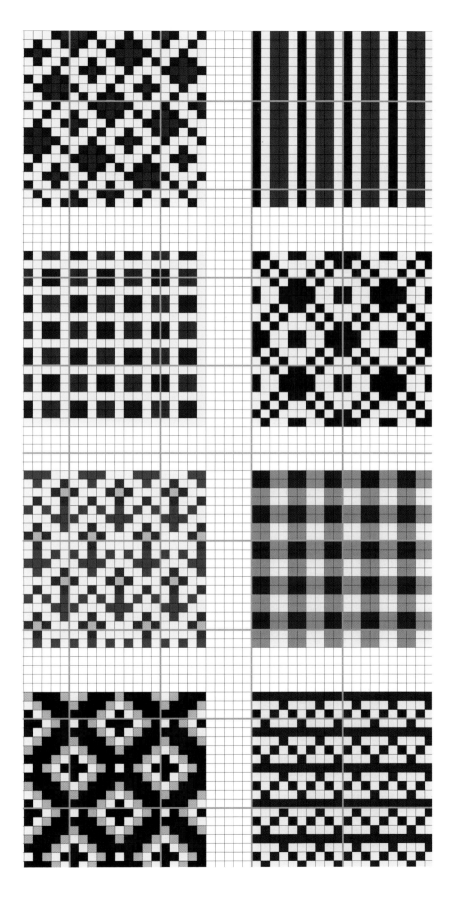

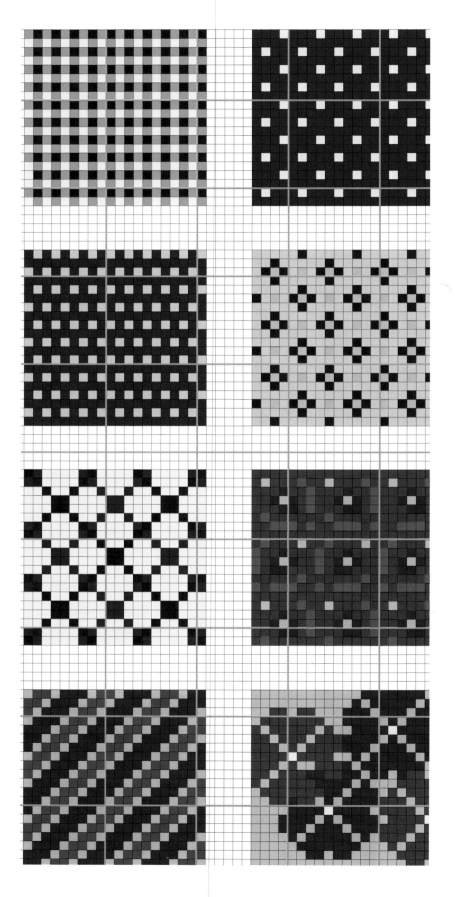

Irish Chain with Flowers

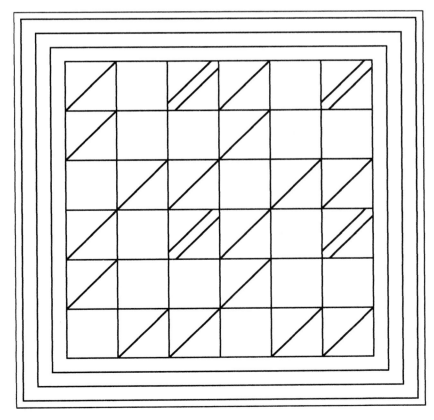

Maple Leaf Rug

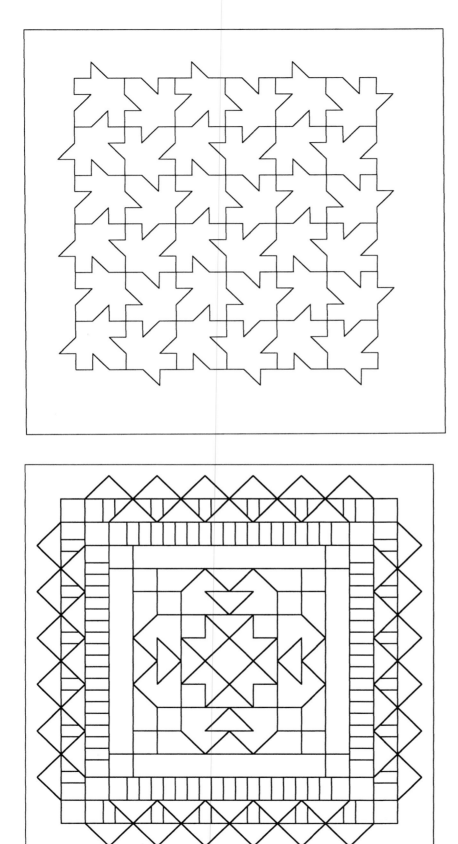

Tessellated Maple Leaf

Shady Pines

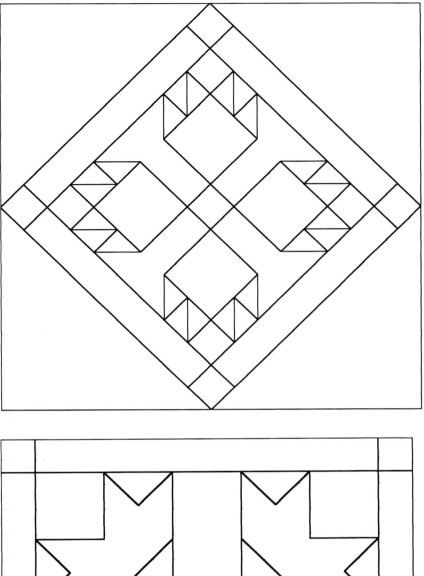

Bear's Paw

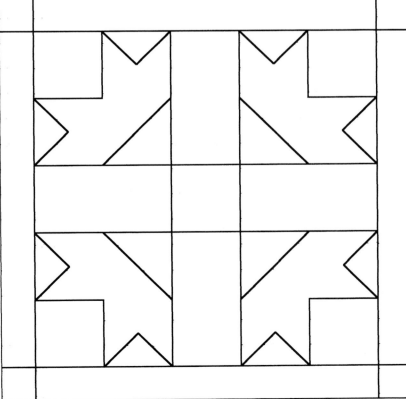

Duck Paddle

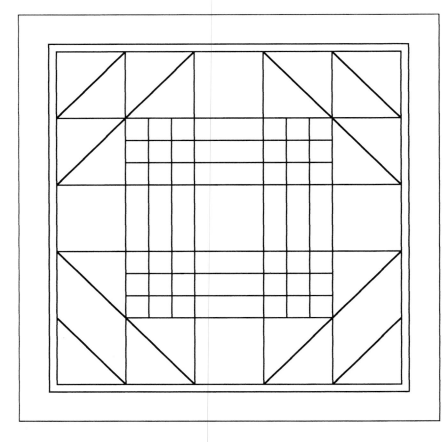

Goose in the Pond

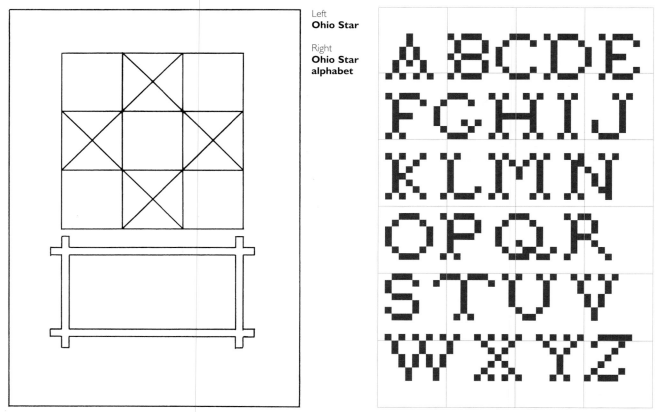

Left
Ohio Star

Right
Ohio Star alphabet

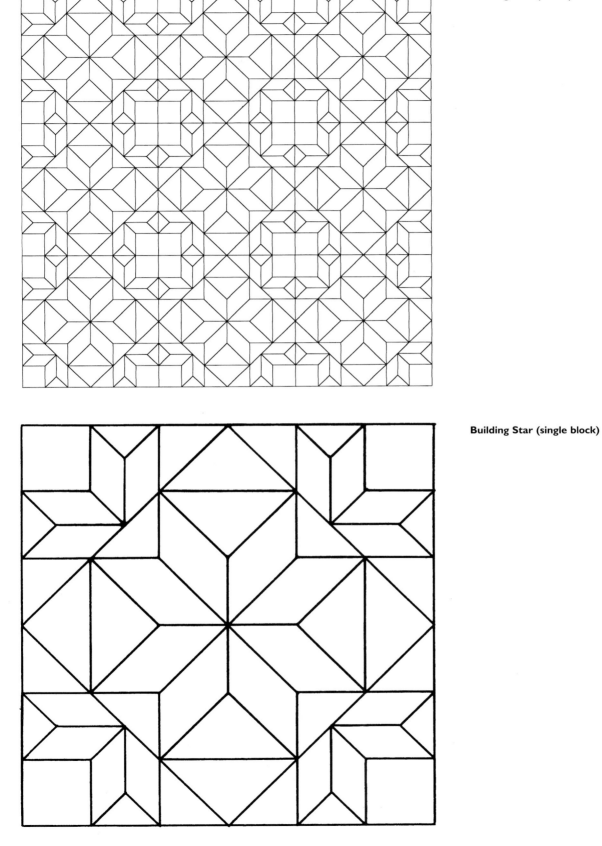

Building Star (whole)

Building Star (single block)

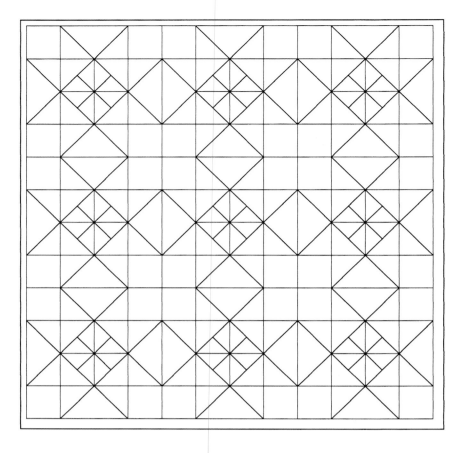

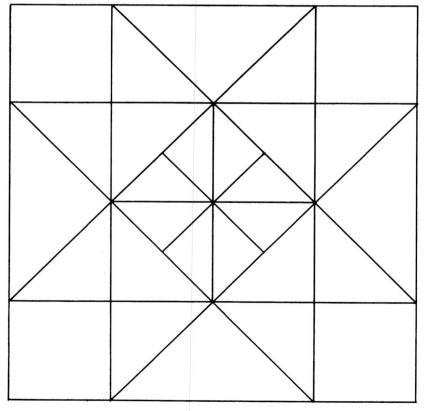

Martha Washington's Star
(single block)

Dutch Rose

Dutch Rose Variation

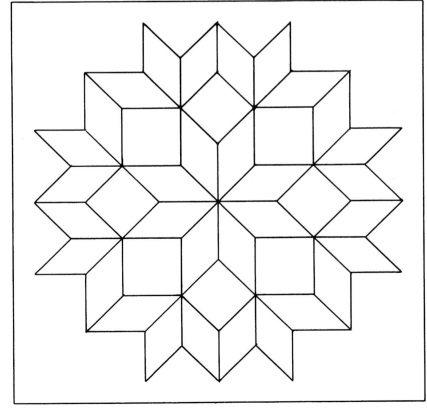

Rainbow Star of Bethlehem

Sunburst

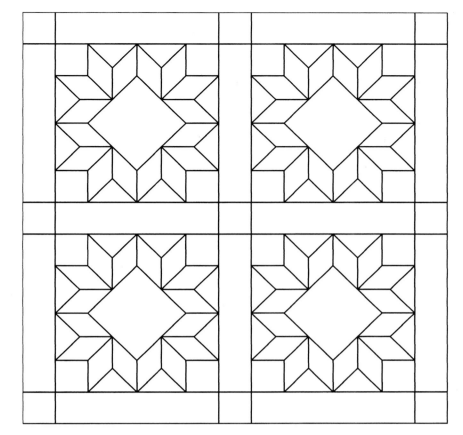

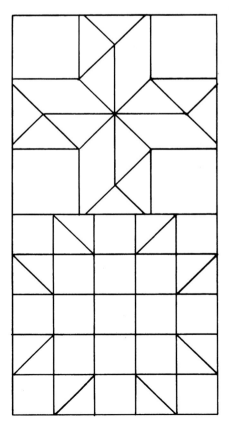

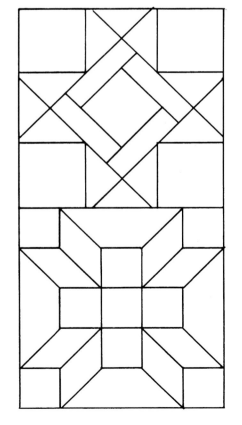

Handy Andy (whole)

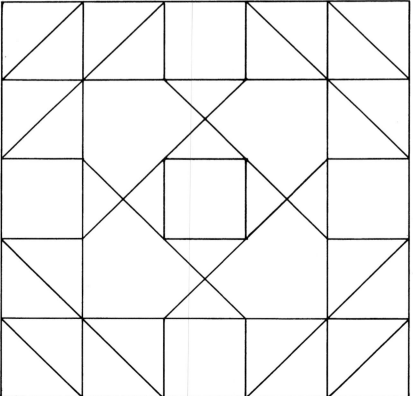

Handy Andy (single block)

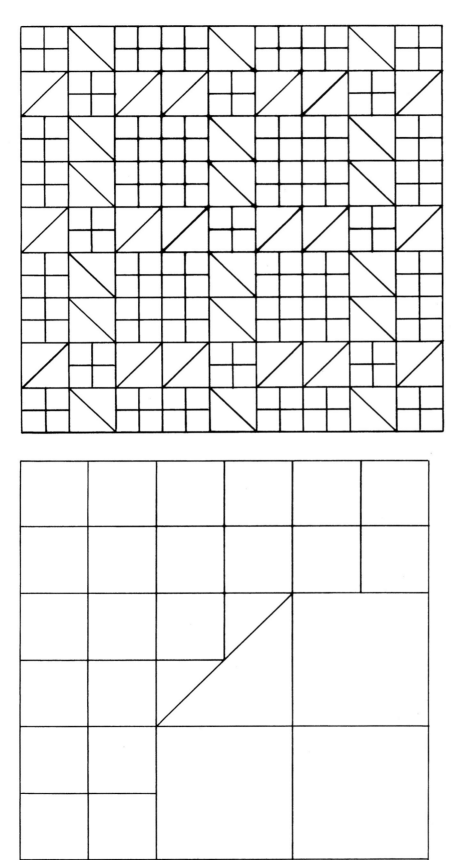

Water Wheel

Steps to the Altar

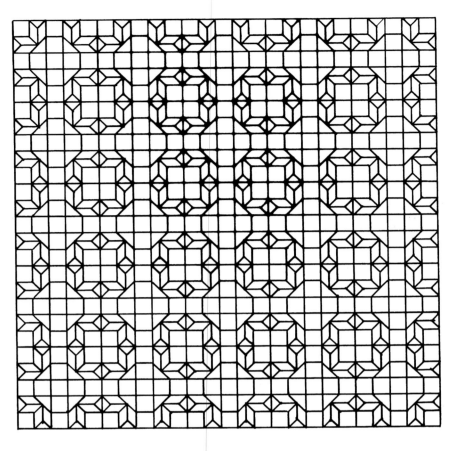

Hands All Round

Arrowhead (whole)

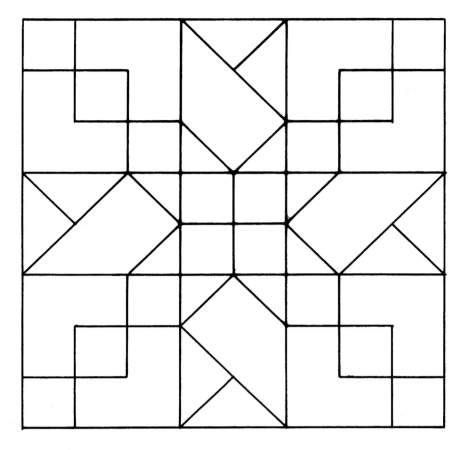

Arrowhead (single block)

House on the Hill

Broken Sash

Basket of Scraps

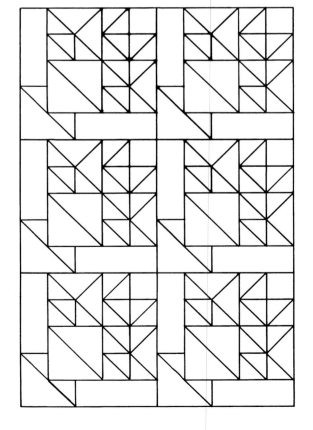

Thread Colour Conversion Tables

Please note that these tables should be used only as a guide, since exact equivalents are not always available. Only colours used in the projects in this book are listed here; the full range is considerably wider.

DMC and Anchor tapestry wools

DMC	Anchor	DMC	Anchor	DMC	Anchor	DMC	Anchor
7030	8630	7313	8776	7448	9602	7709	8590
7037	8806	7314	8672	7449	8354	7746	8034
7038	8808	7318	8632	7452	9442	7759	8368
7055	8018	7319	8634	7459	9542	7760	8396
7056	8098	7320	9006	7469	9648	7780	8102
7057	8124	7327	8882	7472	8056	7782	8100
7058	8022	7329	8884	7474	8024	7783	8024
7106	8214	7344	9100	7492	9322	7784	8098
7108	8218	7354	8368	7499	9430	7785	8096
7110	8220	7356	8260	7503	8054	7796	8692
7124	8258	7360	8162	7505	8100	7798	8644
7137	8442	7364	9202	7511	9326	7799	8684
7139	8424	7369	9014	7520	9654	7800	8682
7147	8402	7370	9004	7533	9648	7801	9646
7169	8264	7377	9264	7535	9666	7823	8694
7171	9504	7379	9208	7544	8218	7860	8924
7184	8240	7385	9008	7547	9166	7909	8970
7196	8368	7387	9024	7548	9164	7918	9524
7198	8242	7389	9026	7579	8052	7920	8236
7208	8424	7393	9264	7595	8822	7922	9536
7212	8422	7398	9182	7596	8922	7943	8972
7245	8596	7402	9074	7600	8458	7946	8194
7247	8612	7408	9028	7602	8456	7947	8166
7288	8838	7417	9268	7604	8962	7954	8984
7297	8838	7424	9258	7606	8198	7961	8400
7298	8814	7428	9024	7650	8822	7971	8120
7299	8742	7429	9028	7666	8202	7973	8118
7303	8236	7436	8122	7677	9286	7995	8808
7304	8790	7439	8164	7679	9282	7999	8906
7306	8792	7444	9526	7690	8900	Blanc	8000
7307	8744	7445	9536	7692	8894	Ecru	8006
7308	8638	7447	8264	7708	8592	Noir	9800

DMC and Anchor stranded cottons

DMC	Anchor
327	101
347	1025
349	13
356	1013
814	45
922	1003
975	357
3350	77

These tables are based on information kindly supplied by Coats Craft UK (manufacturers of Anchor threads) and used with their permission.

Metric Conversion Table

Inches to millimetres and centimetres						
inches	mm	cm	inches	cm	inches	cm
⅛	3	0.3	9	22.9	30	76.2
¼	6	0.6	10	25.4	31	78.7
⅜	10	1.0	11	27.9	32	81.3
½	13	1.3	12	30.5	33	83.8
⅝	16	1.6	13	33.0	34	86.4
¾	19	1.9	14	35.6	35	88.9
⅞	22	2.2	15	38.1	36	91.4
1	25	2.5	16	40.6	37	94.0
1¼	32	3.2	17	43.2	38	96.5
1½	38	3.8	18	45.7	39	99.1
1¾	44	4.4	19	48.3	40	101.6
2	51	5.1	20	50.8	41	104.1
2½	64	6.4	21	53.3	42	106.7
3	76	7.6	22	55.9	43	109.2
3½	89	8.9	23	58.4	44	111.8
4	102	10.2	24	61.0	45	114.3
4½	114	11.4	25	63.5	46	116.8
5	127	12.7	26	66.0	47	119.4
6	152	15.2	27	68.6	48	121.9
7	178	17.8	28	71.1	49	124.5
8	203	20.3	29	73.7	50	127.0

Bibliography

Alistair Cooke's America.
London: BBC Publications, 1973.
ISBN 0-563-12182-3

The Perfect Patchwork Primer.
Beth Gutcheon. UK edition,
Harmondsworth:
Penguin Books, 1973.
ISBN 0-14046-212-0

*Early American Patchwork Quilt
Designs.* Susan Johnston.
Mineola, New York:
Dover Publications, 1984.
ISBN 0-486-24583-7

*Quiltmaking in America: Beyond
the Myths.* The American Quilt
Study Group. Nashville,
Tennessee: Rutledge Hill Press,
1994.
ISBN 1-55853-319-2

*Plain and Fancy: Vermont's People
and their Quilts as a Reflection of
America.* Richard L. Cleveland
and Donna Bister. Gualala,
California: The Quilt Digest
Press, 1991.
ISBN 0-913327-30-1

*The History of the Patchwork
Quilt.* Schnuppe von Gwimmer.
English edition, West Chester,
Pennsylvania: Schiffer Publishing
Ltd, 1988.
ISBN 0-88740-136-8

*Rags to Rainbows: Patchwork
Quilts and Appliqué.* Miranda
Innes. London: Collins and
Brown, 1992.
ISBN 1-85585-145-8

About the Author

Melanie Tacon was born in Manchester, but has lived in south-east England since the age of six.

With no formal artistic education since taking A levels, she is self-taught in all aspects of needlework and textile production, and believes firmly in the exchange and combination of ideas and techniques between the various different disciplines. She has been designing for many years and draws inspirations from nature, architecture, and history.

After a varied career, Melanie now works in computer support within the television industry, and commutes from her home in deepest rural Essex near the river Blackwater.

American Patchwork Designs in Needlepoint is her first book.

Stockists

Threads

DMC Creative World Ltd,
Pullman Road, Wigston,
Leics., LE18 2DY.
0116 281 1040

Anchor threads:
Coats Craft UK,
PO Box 22, The Lingfield Estate,
McMullen Road, Darlington,
Co. Durham, DL1 1QY.
01325 365 457

Canvas

If you experience difficulties in
obtaining canvas, you should
contact DMC on the above
number for your nearest stockist.

Card blanks

Craft Creations Ltd,
1e Ingersoll House,
Delamere Road, Cheshunt,
Herts., EN8 9ND.
01992 781 900 enquiries
01992 781 903 free catalogue

See also Impress Cards and Craft
Materials, below.

Wooden articles: pincushion bases, stools, work boxes, etc.

Both these manufacturers have a
range of beautiful ready-made
articles for sale, but will also
custom-make pieces to fit your
stitching.

Canopia (NC),
PO Box 420, Uxbridge,
Middlesex, UB8 2GW.
01895 235 005

Design Woodcraft, Wing Farm,
Longbridge Deverill,
Warminster, Wilts., BA12 7DD.
01985 841 041

Craft accessories

The following two companies
supply a wide range of needlework and craft accessories by
mail order, including the wooden
boxes used for the Log Cabin
and Crazy Patchwork projects
(Impress), and the bellpull ends
(Framecraft) used for the Mixed
Star Block sampler project
Their products are also widely
available in good needlework
shops.

Impress Cards and Craft
Materials, Slough Farm,
Halesworth,
Suffolk, IP19 8RN.
01986 781 422

Framecraft Miniatures,
372–376 Summer Lane,
Hockley, Birmingham, B19 3QA.
0121 212 0551

Photograph album

The photograph album used in
the Blue Heart project came
from my local branch of
W. H. Smith and Son.

Personal recommendations

Creativity,
45 New Oxford Street,
London WC1A 1BH.
0171 240 2945.

This, in my experience, is the
best-stocked needlework shop in
central London. They will
supply even small quantities by
mail order (including overseas),
and offer a professional stretching service. Their staff are
consistently helpful, pleasant,
and extremely knowledgeable.

My thanks also go to the ladies
at my local needlework shop:
Peachey Ethknits,
6–7 Edwards Walk, Maldon,
Essex. 01621 857 102

Textile Holiday Courses in
Brittany with Gill Thompson.
Send s.a.e. for a brochure to
'Fabric and Threads Plus',
9 Hendre Gardens,
Cardiff, CF5 2HU.

Index

Titles available from
GMC Publications

BOOKS

Woodworking

40 More Woodworking Plans & Projects	*GMC Publications*	Making Little Boxes from Wood	*John Bennett*
Bird Boxes and Feeders for the Garden	*Dave Mackenzie*	Making Shaker Furniture	*Barry Jackson*
Complete Woodfinishing	*Ian Hosker*	Pine Furniture Projects for the Home	*Dave Mackenzie*
Electric Woodwork	*Jeremy Broun*	*The Router* and *Furniture & Cabinetmaking*	
Furniture & Cabinetmaking Projects	*GMC Publications*	Test Reports	*GMC Publications*
Furniture Projects	*Rod Wales*	Sharpening Pocket Reference Book	*Jim Kingshott*
Furniture Restoration (Practical Crafts)	*Kevin Jan Bonner*	Sharpening: The Complete Guide	*Jim Kingshott*
Furniture Restoration and Repair for Beginners	*Kevin Jan Bonner*	Space-Saving Furniture Projects	*Dave Mackenzie*
Green Woodwork	*Mike Abbott*	Stickmaking: A Complete Course	*Andrew Jones & Clive George*
The Incredible Router	*Jeremy Broun*	Veneering: A Complete Course	*Ian Hosker*
Making & Modifying Woodworking Tools	*Jim Kingshott*	Woodfinishing Handbook (Practical Crafts)	*Ian Hosker*
Making Chairs and Tables	*GMC Publications*	Woodworking Plans and Projects	*GMC Publications*
Making Fine Furniture	*Tom Darby*	The Workshop	*Jim Kingshott*

Woodturning

Adventures in Woodturning	*David Springett*	Practical Tips for Turners & Carvers	*GMC Publications*
Bert Marsh: Woodturner	*Bert Marsh*	Practical Tips for Woodturners	*GMC Publications*
Bill Jones' Notes from the Turning Shop	*Bill Jones*	Spindle Turning	*GMC Publications*
Bill Jones' Further Notes from the Turning Shop	*Bill Jones*	Turning Miniatures in Wood	*John Sainsbury*
Colouring Techniques for Woodturners	*Jan Sanders*	Turning Wooden Toys	*Terry Lawrence*
The Craftsman Woodturner	*Peter Child*	Understanding Woodturning	*Ann & Bob Phillips*
Decorative Techniques for Woodturners	*Hilary Bowen*	Useful Techniques for Woodturners	*GMC Publications*
Essential Tips for Woodturners	*GMC Publications*	Useful Woodturning Projects	*GMC Publications*
Faceplate Turning	*GMC Publications*	Woodturning: A Foundation Course	*Keith Rowley*
Fun at the Lathe	*R.C. Bell*	Woodturning: A Source Book of Shapes	*John Hunnex*
Illustrated Woodturning Techniques	*John Hunnex*	Woodturning Jewellery	*Hilary Bowen*
Intermediate Woodturning Projects	*GMC Publications*	Woodturning Masterclass	*Tony Boase*
Keith Rowley's Woodturning Projects	*Keith Rowley*	Woodturning Techniques	*GMC Publications*
Make Money from Woodturning	*Ann & Bob Phillips*	*Woodturning* Tools & Equipment Test Reports	*GMC Publications*
Multi-Centre Woodturning	*Ray Hopper*	Woodturning Wizardry	*David Springett*
Pleasure and Profit from Woodturning	*Reg Sherwin*		

Woodcarving

The Art of the Woodcarver	*GMC Publications*	Understanding Woodcarving in the Round	*GMC Publications*
Carving Birds & Beasts	*GMC Publications*	Useful Techniques for Woodcarvers	*GMC Publications*
Carving on Turning	*Chris Pye*	Wildfowl Carving - Volume 1	*Jim Pearce*
Carving Realistic Birds	*David Tippey*	Wildfowl Carving - Volume 2	*Jim Pearce*
Decorative Woodcarving	*Jeremy Williams*	The Woodcarvers	*GMC Publications*
Essential Tips for Woodcarvers	*GMC Publications*	Woodcarving: A Complete Course	*Ron Butterfield*
Essential Woodcarving Techniques	*Dick Onians*	Woodcarving: A Foundation Course	*Zoë Gertner*
Lettercarving in Wood: A Practical Course	*Chris Pye*	Woodcarving for Beginners	*GMC Publications*
Practical Tips for Turners & Carvers	*GMC Publications*	*Woodcarving* Tools & Equipment Test Reports	*GMC Publications*
Relief Carving in Wood: A Practical Introduction	*Chris Pye*	Woodcarving Tools, Materials & Equipment	*Chris Pye*
Understanding Woodcarving	*GMC Publications*		

Upholstery

Seat Weaving (Practical Crafts)	*Ricky Holdstock*	Upholstery Restoration	*David James*
Upholsterer's Pocket Reference Book	*David James*	Upholstery Techniques & Projects	*David James*
Upholstery: A Complete Course	*David James*		

Toymaking

Designing & Making Wooden Toys — *Terry Kelly*
Fun to Make Wooden Toys & Games — *Jeff & Jennie Loader*
Making Board, Peg & Dice Games — *Jeff & Jennie Loader*
Making Wooden Toys & Games — *Jeff & Jennie Loader*

Restoring Rocking Horses — *Clive Green & Anthony Dew*
Scrollsaw Toy Projects — *Ivor Carlyle*
Wooden Toy Projects — *GMC Publications*

Dolls' Houses and Miniatures

Architecture for Dolls' Houses — *Joyce Percival*
Beginners' Guide to the Dolls' House Hobby — *Jean Nisbett*
The Complete Dolls' House Book — *Jean Nisbett*
Dolls' House Accessories, Fixtures and Fittings — *Andrea Barham*
Dolls' House Bathrooms: Lots of Little Loos — *Patricia King*
Easy to Make Dolls' House Accessories — *Andrea Barham*
Make Your Own Dolls' House Furniture — *Maurice Harper*
Making Dolls' House Furniture — *Patricia King*
Making Georgian Dolls' Houses — *Derek Rowbottom*
Making Miniature Oriental Rugs & Carpets — *Meik & Ian*

McNaughton
Making Period Dolls' House Accessories — *Andrea Barham*
Making Period Dolls' House Furniture — *Derek & Sheila Rowbottom*
Making Tudor Dolls' Houses — *Derek Rowbottom*
Making Unusual Miniatures — *Graham Spalding*
Making Victorian Dolls' House Furniture — *Patricia King*
Miniature Bobbin Lace — *Roz Snowden*
Miniature Embroidery for the Victorian Dolls' House — *Pamela Warner*
Miniature Needlepoint Carpets — *Janet Granger*

Crafts

American Patchwork Designs in Needlepoint — *Melanie Tacon*
A Beginners' Guide to Rubber Stamping — *Brenda Hunt*
Celtic Knotwork Designs — *Sheila Sturrock*
Collage from Seeds, Leaves and Flowers — *Joan Carver*
Complete Pyrography — *Stephen Poole*
Creating Knitwear Designs — *Pat Ashforth & Steve Plummer*
Creative Embroidery Techniques Using
    Colour Through Gold — *Daphne J. Ashby & Jackie Woolsey*
Cross Stitch Kitchen Projects — *Janet Granger*
Cross Stitch on Colour — *Sheena Rogers*

Embroidery Tips & Hints — *Harold Hayes*
An Introduction to Crewel Embroidery — *Mave Glenny*
Making Character Bears — *Valerie Tyler*
Making Greetings Cards for Beginners — *Pat Sutherland*
Making Knitwear Fit — *Pat Ashforth & Steve Plummer*
Needlepoint: A Foundation Course — *Sandra Hardy*
Pyrography Handbook (Practical Crafts) — *Stephen Poole*
Tassel Making for Beginners — *Enid Taylor*
Tatting Collage — *Lindsay Rogers*
Temari: A Traditional Japanese Embroidery Technique — *Margaret Ludlow*

The Home

Home Ownership: Buying and Maintaining — *Nicholas Snelling*

Security for the Householder: Fitting Locks and Other Devices — *E. Phillips*

VIDEOS

Drop-in and Pinstuffed Seats — *David James*
Stuffover Upholstery — *David James*
Elliptical Turning — *David Springett*
Woodturning Wizardry — *David Springett*
Turning Between Centres: The Basics — *Dennis White*
Turning Bowls — *Dennis White*
Boxes, Goblets and Screw Threads — *Dennis White*
Novelties and Projects — *Dennis White*
Classic Profiles — *Dennis White*

Twists and Advanced Turning — *Dennis White*
Sharpening the Professional Way — *Jim Kingshott*
Sharpening Turning & Carving Tools — *Jim Kingshott*
Bowl Turning — *John Jordan*
Hollow Turning — *John Jordan*
Woodturning: A Foundation Course — *Keith Rowley*
Carving a Figure: The Female Form — *Ray Gonzalez*
The Router: A Beginner's Guide — *Alan Goodsell*
The Scroll Saw: A Beginner's Guide — *John Burke*

MAGAZINES

Woodturning • Woodcarving • Furniture & Cabinetmaking • The Router
The Dolls' House Magazine • Creative Crafts for the Home • BusinessMatters

---

The above represents a full list of all titles currently published or scheduled to be published.
All are available direct from the Publishers or through bookshops, newsagents and specialist retailers.
To place an order, or to obtain a complete catalogue, contact:
GMC Publications,
166 High Street, Lewes, East Sussex BN7 1XU, United Kingdom Tel: 01273 488005 Fax: 01273 478606
Orders by credit card are accepted